T0322193

JUST GOOD MANNERS

Also by William Hanson

Bluffer's Guide to Etiquette
Bluffer's Guide to Entertaining
Protocol to Manage Relationships Today *(co-author)*
Help I S*xted My Boss *(with Jordan North)*

William Hanson

JUST GOOD MANNERS

A Quintessential
Guide to Courtesy,
Charm, Grace
and Decorum

C

CENTURY

7 9 10 8 6

Century
20 Vauxhall Bridge Road
London SW1V 2SA

Century is part of the Penguin Random House group of companies
whose addresses can be found at global.penguinrandomhouse.com

Penguin
Random House
UK

Copyright © William Hanson, 2024

William Hanson has asserted his right to be identified as the author of this
Work in accordance with the Copyright, Designs and Patents Act 1988

Illustrations © Alice Tait, 2024

Line on p. 35 from 'It's Raining Men', recorded by The Weather Girls (1982);
written by Paul Jabara and Paul Shaffer (1979)

Line on p. 38 from 'How About You?', recorded by Frank Sinatra and
Tommy Dorsey (1942); lyrics by Ralph Freed (1941)

First published by Century in 2024

www.penguin.co.uk

A CIP catalogue record for this book is available from the British Library

ISBN 9781529939958

Typeset in 12/14.75pt Dante MT Std by Jouve (UK), Milton Keynes
Printed and bound in Great Britain by Clays Ltd, Elcograf S.p.A.

The authorised representative in the EEA is Penguin Random House Ireland,
Morrison Chambers, 32 Nassau Street, Dublin D02 YH68

www.greenpenguin.co.uk

MIX
Paper | Supporting
responsible forestry
FSC
www.fsc.org
FSC® C018179

Penguin Random House is committed to a
sustainable future for our business, our readers
and our planet. This book is made from Forest
Stewardship Council® certified paper.

To Granny, who gave me the etiquette book
that launched a thousand ships.

'When in Rome, do as the British do.'

Audrey fforbes-Hamilton, *To the Manor Born*

Contents

Preface

In Britain, no social issue is bigger than whether cream or jam is the first to be added to a scone. The second biggest is the pronunciation of the word 'scone' – it rhymes with 'gone', by the way. Don't argue – the King says it like that, and it's his English.

If I had a pound for every time I have been asked by a journalist, a student or a correspondent on social media what my take on the jam-versus-cream debate is, I would not be writing this book. I would be far too busy getting expensively bronzed and preparing to host an al fresco dinner at my Messelian villa on Mustique.

Every six months or so, the cream/jam debate comes back around in the British press, often prompted by the actions of someone of note. During the electioneering of 2015, the then prime minister David Cameron visited a cafe in Barnstaple, Devon, and pronounced that, in Devon, you add jam first and then cream to scones – which, for those new to this matter of life and death, is the Cornish way, not the Devonian. This was a very serious breach of local custom. You can imagine the uproar. It's a miracle he wasn't removed from office and terrorised by the clotted-cream resistance faction, known as the OoRA. William and Catherine – who, please note, currently hold the titles of Duke and Duchess of Cornwall – weighed into the clotted-cream quagmire in 2023. Catherine said she preferred cream last, while William remained diplomatic and didn't give an explicit answer. Devon and Cornwall are the lead producers of clotted cream, and, aside from their dairy production, these two most south-westerly counties in England famously like to find ways to annoy each other. I suspect their distinct edicts on where to stick the cream came about as an example of this.

When I teach afternoon-tea etiquette, which sometimes is several times a day (in 2014, I had seventy-two teas), I aver that if you are eating a scone in Devon, do cream first, and if you are in Cornwall, cream last. If you are elsewhere in the world, do it however you so please. Like the Prince of Wales, I prefer to be neutral and suggest doing one half one way, and the other half the other.*

Brits from the south-west reading this may have possibly thrown the book across the room, because I have not decreed that one way is preferable to the other. It's a weird quirk of British etiquette that we have decided such a little detail matters, and that those who disagree are to be treated with great suspicion. But it is representative of the eccentricities of our nation's behavioural codes and customs.

In a similar vein, I was once away for work, deep in Riyadh. I was there to teach international business protocol at a leading Saudi bank – then a twice-annual booking. That particular afternoon's session took an unusual turn when, during a scheduled discussion on boardroom seating dynamics, one of the twelve graduates (it was always ten men and two women) queried why I had just flagged, as a passing thought, that in Britain none of us would be able to sit down to eat together, as we were a group of thirteen.

'But why should that be an issue?' I was gently interrogated.

'Well, Abdulaziz, in Britain we say that thirteen cannot sit down for any lunch or dinner, or else one of the party may die.' Only

---

* Incidentally, the island of Jersey also produces very good clotted cream. They have no strong feeling either way on whether it goes before or after the jam, just so long as it's taxed as little as possible.

after being rechallenged on this did I have a heart-in-mouth moment when I realised I was about to start extemporising about the New Testament in a deeply conservative Muslim country.

But, to both my surprise and my relief, after I had carefully explained how there were thirteen during the 'last supper' and that this had led to Judas's betrayal of Jesus and the latter's crucifixion, none of the group seemed bothered by my synoptic summary. Instead, my pragmatic students wanted to know how we in Britain coped at Christmas if, by chance, there were thirteen in the family. Did we disinvite Granny? Did we build a second dining room?

'No, it's perfectly simple,' I started with a broad smile. 'What some British families do is that we set the table for fourteen people, get an old teddy bear from the nursery, and we pop it on the four-teenth chair and invite the teddy to join us for lunch.'

As I stopped talking, I surveyed my students' stunned faces. They clearly thought that I, along with those in Britain who would do this, had completely lost the plot. To me, and I dare say to many native British readers, the teddy bear solution seems perfectly normal and rational. Teddies are part of the family – in fact, many traditional British ('trad Brits') give more love and affection to their Steiffs than their actual blood relatives. Only when I had to explain this bear-on-the-chair to my Arab cohort did I realise that, on paper, it is completely ludicrous.*

---

* Since 1920, The Savoy has had Kaspar, a black wooden cat that is placed in a fourteenth seat should thirteen sit down to eat. The cat replaced the work-around the hotel had previously been using, of having a waiter take the fourteenth place. Architect Basil Ionides created Kaspar during a renovation of the private dining room. Why he picked a cat, no one knows, but to this day the cat sits in the hotel's lobby, ready to be put to use to avoid the untimely death of a diner.

Whether it's the order for scone toppings, pronunciation debates or teddy bears, British manners are a bit weird. Weird but wonderful. While Italy may hold the crown for food and art, France for fashion and Germany for efficient engineering, in Britain we can just about still wear the crown for courtesy. Over many centuries, we Brits have taken hold of general good manners and put our own layer of politesse over the top, making us the market leader in the subject.

Thank heavens I was born in Britain and that I do the job I do. As I have no talents in life except teaching etiquette, it would have been tricky to be from anywhere else. Can you imagine if I had been born in Australia, and rocked up to teach napkin-folding to a tech start-up in Wagga Wagga? Or if I were Norwegian, and dared try to discuss how to split a scone in Fredrikstad? I'm just not sure it would have worked.

There are, of course, excellent etiquette consultants in both countries who do a sterling job, but I'm not sure the Saudis would have asked an Aussie or a Norwegian to go all that way to talk business etiquette. My nationality has made my work life a lot easier.

Teaching etiquette was not a career I set out to pursue initially. Just before my grandmother gave her slightly precocious eldest grandson his first etiquette book, I had been considering a career either reading the news, entering the world of espionage, or as the Archbishop of Canterbury (not for any particular religious reason, but the vestments looked quite fun). But my life began to change once I opened my copy of John Morgan's offering for Debrett's. Suddenly there was a subject that was staying put in my head. I struggled to remember anything our history teacher was saying about Pobedonostsev, and I failed to muster any enthusiasm for trigonometry, but my brain fired on all cylinders when it came to learning that, for a buffet, a tablecloth must be to the floor.

Knowing these rules and guidelines appealed to my precious nature, and helped me gain an edge over my peers. We were all meant to know about Russian statesmen and maths equations, but I wanted to be different and have the advantage of etiquette.

As great as John Morgan's book was – and if this book is a tenth as good as his, I will be delighted – it posed lots of questions for twelve-year-old William. It was all very well for Mr Morgan to tell us the rules, but some clarification or explanation would have been nice. I started to buy more books on etiquette, reading around the subject, and luckily began to get some answers.

My interest in the subject has since become all-consuming. Not a moment goes by when I am not pondering the polite. Indeed, the brilliant Camilla Long of the *Sunday Times* once described me as 'utterly consumed by napkins and the correct sort of loafer'. It means I can't ever really switch off, be deliberately rude to someone, or walk to the post box in my pyjamas. When I am rude to someone – always unintentionally – as both a manners maven and a Brit I often dive into a catastrophic spiral of panic. When one spends their life advising others on the correct course of action and how best to do things, any transgression of this, especially when completely unintentional, is akin to breaching the law.

Even though many think of what I do as niche, it's not. Passing on instruction in the correct way to do things is a very old profession – albeit not as old as some. While the men of the eighteenth century were galivanting around Europe on their 'grand tours', learning about the arts, gambling, sex and finance, their female counterparts were 'finished' at home. Think about Dickens's Mrs General (from *Little Dorrit*) who, although fictitious, is a dramatic embodiment of widowed women of a certain age who were brought in by aspirational families to help polish their charges, who were about to launch themselves onto the social scene and the marriage market.

The late nineteenth century saw the rise of finishing schools. Thanks to the Industrial Revolution, the middle class of Britain had expanded tenfold. Daughters from these newly aspirational families were sent to learn critically vital life skills, such as how to laugh to a scale, get in and out of a carriage while protecting their modesty, and where to stick a hardy perennial red-hot poker. And it wasn't just Britain that had such schools. Many European countries did too. Switzerland arguably led the way, offering Alpine entertainment and tuition on the slopes, and the Swiss culture of consensus gave them the edge over their competitors. Once girls had passed through these finishing schools and their rigorous academic standards, they were eligible for marriage.

Finishing schools survived well into the twentieth century, the most famous British institutions being Winkfield Place and Lucie Clayton's – the latter of which clung on until the 1990s, when it began to focus on secretarial and business skills. As a result, the finishing and etiquette side was absorbed into The English Manner, a company I am now proud to own and run. Other than Institut Villa Pierrefeu in Switzerland, which remains in operation today, the schools in Britain and Europe wilted as most of them never updated their curriculum to reflect the society around them and the rise in the equality of the sexes from the 1960s onwards.* Those poor girls were still toying with red-hot pokers while the carriages had been switched for motorcars and The Beatles were making miniskirted girls scream as they adjusted their Quants ever upwards.

---

* Institut Villa Pierrefeu opened in 1954, moving to Montreux in 1965. Principal Mme Viviane Neri has a good take on the role of finishing schools and etiquette institutions: 'We don't finish anyone: we start them by giving them tools that regular schools have not and open their eyes to the benefits of multicultural social interaction.'

For centuries, Britain led the way in educating the world in manners, not just through etiquette education but by producing books that offered advice on 'the done thing', such as the *Boke of Curtasye* (1440), *Youth's Behaviour; or, Decency in Conversation Among Men* (1640), Philip Stanhope's *Letters to His Son on the Art of Becoming a Gentleman* (1774), and more recently when Debrett's, who up until the 1980s had only collated the names and lineage of living aristocracy to produce a glorified Yellow Pages, entered the etiquette publishing world with their first guide, authored by Elsie Burch Donald.

Dare I say that maybe even the former British Empire and its diplomats contributed to holding up our mantle as etiquette tutors to the world. While France and Italy also sought to codify standards of behaviour, they bloodily got rid of their royal families – while ours survives, and those within it still conduct themselves with grace and poise despite the odd spectacular blip here and there.

But are the British and our manners the envy or joke of other nations? Recently, I was posted to Oman for six weeks on an assignment working with the Diwan (the royal court). Together with Jean Paul, my Dutch colleague, we decided that given the nature of our work and the ongoing pandemic, we should let our respective ambassadors know we would be in Muscat, the country's capital, for a longer-than-normal period of time. As it happened, our emails crossed.

I opened Jean Paul's missive to the Dutch ambassador. 'Dear Laetitia,' it efficiently and casually began. I winced. He'd never met her! A first-name basis? The cheek of it. A few scant, matter-of-fact lines about our posting followed, before the unceremonious sign-off 'Yours sincerely, Jean Paul'. Yours sincerely?! That's how I might close an email to the council about a missed bin collection, not how one should communicate with the permanent representative of a royal head of state.

xvii

Cut to my email to the British ambassador, which struck a remarkably more formal tone. 'Your Excellency,' it began. I was genuflecting as low as I could go as I typed. Umpteen waffly paragraphs followed, over-explaining everything Jean Paul had managed to express in just a few concise sentences, before my big finish. I concluded (deep breath): 'I have the honour to be, with the highest consideration, Your Excellency's obedient servant.' I was now metaphorically prostrate on the floor.

Funnily enough, someone from the British Embassy only got back to me on the penultimate day of our six-week trip; the ambassador of the Netherlands personally replied to Jean Paul within thirty-six hours. But at least I knew I had followed protocol.

What did Jean Paul make of my obsequious email? Did he feel bad about his informality, or did he forward the email to his colleagues to show how weird we are in Britain? We've always done deference quite well in Britain, of course. We may not be as deferential as we once were – the sexual and social revolutions of the 1960s saw to that – but when it comes to terms of address and noting rank, we still lead the way.

My British audience has always been the trickiest throughout my career. When I teach in China, it's a much easier 'act' to perform, as I've found they will sit there and listen diligently, perhaps thanks to their more intense educational conditioning. I've never needed to resort to jokes or witty asides. If anything, it's a bit dull for me. Brits really do need a spoonful of sugar to help the mannerly medicine go down. And should gentle teasing and arch humour not work, Brits love history. Why do we do it, who made us do it, and for how long have we been doing it that way?

Further modification is needed when I teach in America, as the history has to be stripped away. When I was in New York City, I referenced the Roman Empire, and one of the students asked if that was the one that ended in late 1800s. Americans are much more training-focused as a nation. Perhaps due to their comparative youth as a country, they don't bristle as much at the thought of group learning or admitting they may not know something.

In Britain, we get so many people who don't want others to know they have had tutorage in manners. I see people who like to appear they know it all, or don't need to learn as the whole thing is a bit beneath them; they have persuaded themselves into thinking we are some uber-egalitarian, laid-back, fancy-free society and don't need to worry about other people and how our actions affect them. Though, not wanting to bad-mouth that sort of person too much, I shall defend them by saying they may have a soupçon of sense. Etiquette has certainly changed since it was most popularly codified in the court of Louis XIV.

Back then, when little signs and labels were placed around palaces like Versailles to keep the patrician paysans in their place, rules were made up to elevate Louis, giving him a godlike aura and excluding others who were so conscious of their behaviour that they'd be on edge – so eager to impress that they wouldn't dream of questioning authority. You couldn't look at the royalty, you couldn't sit in front of royalty or speak until you were spoken to. I'm told life is still like that today for those living and working in a certain house in Montecito. But with the exception of that 18,000-square-foot, sixteen-bathroomed mansion in California, etiquette today is – when used correctly – much more *inclusive*. A change which anyone can track by reading the tomes of correct behaviour published over the last few hundred years.

In my eyes, etiquette manuals throughout history have two main uses. Their primary function at the time of their writing was to help lubricate social interactions with fellow human beings. Many believe that children generally do better with rules and frameworks within which to live; adults are no different. Their second function, which only becomes apparent years later, is to reflect how life was at that point, to educate and inform future generations. Some of my naysayers think my colleagues and I only teach people a code of conduct from the court of George III, or – if we're feeling modern – that we advocate for a return to Victorian manners. What they don't see is the evolution of etiquette – how it's a malleable shapeshifter that must always adapt to the society of the day. Etiquette is as much about addressing an ambassador as it is about brushing off something objectionable someone might have said – a perennial issue, but one we seem to encounter more today.

Things we may have grown up learning are correct may become incorrect as life moves on. I used to have quite fascist views on doggie bags, but have since had an epiphany that in an age of obscene food waste and with many in life starving, they are actually marvellous – but only if the restaurant offers one (it's still not great form to ask).

In these pages, I have tried to find a sensible balance between what has been accepted for many years (much of which either is still correct or can be easily adapted to life today), what is a load of outdated rubbish, and where new gaps in knowledge needed to be filled.

You may use as much or as little as you like of what follows in this book. Use it to add some finesse to your already wonderful life, to laugh along with your fellow Brits – or, if you aren't British yourself, you might use it to understand us and how we behave today.

CHAPTER ONE

A Manifesto for Manners

I will now mount my soapbox.

Etiquette and good manners are needed more than ever. You can't scroll through a news app or swipe on social media without seeing someone attacking someone else, being discourteous or not doing the right thing. Culprits will argue that civility is no longer relevant, and that we are now in a totally different world where anything goes. Personal choice and freedom have, they say, replaced the need for observing the little courtesies and pleasantries. It's dog-eat-dog. But I contend that the people who make this argument are (badly) trying to disguise their own ignorance of the rules and accepted norms. They probably fail to realise that many of the principles of good manners have evolved over time. Some have been adjusted with trial and error, others by common sense, and the rest have their origins in our rich history. However they have been formed, most of the principles of politeness will outlast the naysayers, because most of us still want to treat others well.

On other occasions, out there in the wilderness, I find specimens who agree that manners are needed, but that etiquette is not. Lunacy! You cannot have manners without etiquette. Yes, they are different, but they are also a married couple. And like any married couple, sometimes they disagree and contradict each other. But, contretemps aside, ultimately they are a unit.

Manners are the guiding principles of putting people at their ease, of not embarrassing others, and of generally putting yourself second. Good manners are selfless, not selfish. All cultures around the globe believe in the importance of good manners. Etiquette, on the other hand, is a set of rules by which a society lives. How you become well-mannered is (nine times out of ten) by following the rules of etiquette. There are times when the rules will not be appropriate, and when actually the politest thing is to do quite the opposite to what the rulebook says . . . But more often than not, the correct etiquette is exactly that – correct! To be the most well-mannered person in the room, you need to know the rules of etiquette and have the confidence to break those rules at the appropriate moment.

There is an apocryphal story, allegedly involving Charles III when he was Prince of Wales. Supposedly, during an official dinner for a visiting dignitary from a developing country, finger food was served and cut-glass finger bowls were set above the forks, as is the custom. Said distinguished guest innocently mistook the finger bowl for his water glass, picked it up and started drinking from it. Some British guests saw and started to quietly laugh and point. Charles, noticing this, picked up his own finger bowl and drank from it to silence them and make the guest of honour feel at ease.

While it is definitely not etiquette to drink from a finger bowl, it is very bad manners to laugh at someone who does, especially when they are from a country where they have more pressing things to worry about than finger-bowl finesse. That same story is told with a variety of protagonists, from Queen Wilhelmina of the

Netherlands to Jacqueline Kennedy, so we may never know who it really was – if it was anyone at all – but being patriotic and shamelessly hoping for a gong one day, I attribute it to our now King.

'Etiquette' has become a loaded word. Its grander French etymology adds some off-putting gilding. It may be hard for someone who has had a far-from-royal upbringing to think they need to observe the rules of etiquette. But every situation involves a code of behaviour, whether people like it or not. It's not just about who is presented to whom at court; it's how to handle break-ups with grace and to let a restaurant know you are still coming the day before. I dare say there is even etiquette around a gangland drug exchange. So long as humans interact with one another, there will be the need for etiquette and manners.

I do accept that some people can use etiquette for improper means, however. The television show *Ladette to Lady* – which briefly aired in America as *The Girls of Hedsor Hall*, executive produced by Donald Trump – was a prime example of etiquette gone rogue. To be fair to those involved, they were victims of the era of car-crash television (although they did go along with it for multiple series). But showing coiffured harridans screaming at Jemma, jailed for flashing her breasts in Faliraki as she exited a hatchback clumsily, was never going to be good PR for politeness.

Shows like these failed to acknowledge that etiquette evolves and changes rather than being frozen in a bygone era. Where it was once about gaining skills to catch a husband or preparing to inherit the family seat, today etiquette helps us progress at work, make friends from all walks of life, and simply become a kind, compassionate person whom others want to be around. Granted, we are using rules that have been around for some time, many of which were codified in a more gilded habitat, but, at their core, they are applicable anywhere.

Some of the etiquette we still use today does originate from a more rarefied environment. Particularly in Britain, it is hard to separate it from social class. Even now, with a far less rigid class structure than in previous centuries, much focus is put on class as we're so obsessed with it – with each of us, whether secretly or openly, aspiring to a perceived greatness (though each person will define greatness in their own way). It's become taboo to acknowledge that we still have a class structure. But the more we talk about something and acknowledge it, gently mocking it where it needs to be mocked, the less of an issue it will be.

During the exploration of modern manners within these pages, there will be many references to 'posh' versus 'common'. Brace yourselves. This is Britain. For readers from this blessed plot, I hate to break it to you, but if you don't like the fact that we have this additional arch and snobby layer to our behaviour codes, you may want to consider emigrating. It's not going to vanish, however much you may want it to. Britain is too much of an old country with a verdant history for it to go. On the other hand, if you take it all too seriously, you are going to give it more weight than it arguably deserves. Much of it is pure snobbery and just a cashmere-covered sociolect, though some of what is dismissed as classism is actually specificity. For instance, a 'toilet' was historically your make-up and appearance, not the white china thing into which you had a wee. That's a 'lavatory' or 'loo'.

The insecure French Sun King, Louis XIV, bequeathed us a fair number of the dining rules followed around the world. In his court, if you dared open your napkin before him, there would be tears before bedtime as you were dropped down the order of precedence. Today, this rule still applies, although hardly anyone will notice if you flick open your napkin a beat too early. (Don't dramatically waft it to one side of you, however, or you might take someone's eye out.)

But as life has morphed into the shape it is currently, new rules have come from 'the people' rather than from the ruling families. I am quite sure that most of the British aristocracy have not given much thought to inclusive language, for example. That's not to say they would disagree with the inclusive reasoning behind it, but as they still have not updated their own primogeniture rules, worrying about pronouns and gender-neutral language is probably nowhere near the top of their agendas.*

The world is very different to how it was in the respective days of *Pride and Prejudice*'s Elizabeth Bennet and *Downton Abbey*'s Lord and Lady Grantham. Thanks to the ease of international travel and the internet, the world has become much smaller, and we interact with people far more often and at a quicker pace than any of our predecessors. Since COVID-19, we easily meet people from all over the world on video calls, driving globalised communication even further than we could have anticipated before the pandemic. While taking the time to do things with courtesy, respect for others and self-respect may slow us down, it is only infinitesimally. And if you know the rules and are confident with them, they become second nature. I always give the analogy of driving a car. Unless you are the next best thing to Lando Norris when you first learn to drive, you will be so worried about keeping the car on the road, and going in a straight

---

* Primogeniture is the right, usually by law, of the firstborn legitimate child to inherit the parent's entire or main estate. In most contexts, it means the inheritance of the firstborn son. There was an attempt to change British law in 2013 with the Equality (Titles) Bill, but it was rejected at committee stage in the House of Lords. The British Royal Family did, however, abolish male-preference primogeniture as of 2015, which is why Princess Charlotte of Wales outranks her younger brother, Prince Louis of Wales. Anne, the Princess Royal, however, is outranked by both her younger brothers (the Duke of York and the Duke of Edinburgh), as the changes were not retrospective and only affect those born after 28 October 2011.

line without hitting any passing pensioners, that you won't be able to make chit-chat with your instructor, have the radio on or check your hair in the mirror. But once you pass your test and have mastered your manoeuvring, all those things become instinctive – and your muscle memory takes over as you change gears and shift lanes. Etiquette should be like that. It is not a restrictive straitjacket to keep people in their place, but a series of tried-and-tested guidelines for an easy life with few crashes.

Contemporary British etiquette is rooted in six key principles.

Humility

Brits do not go in for shameless self-promotion. Indeed, many of us struggle to talk about ourselves in a positive light. This does not mean we lack self-worth, having been raised with very little praise or outward displays of love (although I am sure, for some people, that plays a part); it just equates to us not wanting other people to think we are being pushy or stepping out of place.

True humility is not merely the absence of arrogance but a refined expression of self-awareness – a knowing understatement that elevates the collective comfort over individual accolades. It is this artful modesty that oils the gears of our social machinery, ensuring that interactions are marked not by brash self-promotion but by a gracious, understated acknowledgement of one's own place and achievements.

Consider my favourite sitcom character, Hyacinth Bucket from *Keeping Up Appearances*. She was funny to those watching, as the endless domestic rodomontade and perpetual varnishing of her life jarred with the usual British way of doing things, even though dear Hyacinth would have said she was British to the core.

8

While other nations may think we are a land of snobs, the humility many display is the opposite of boasting about achievements and triumphs, and making others feel like they have not achieved the same greatness. There is something very satisfying about the quiet confidence of knowing that you are right about something but not announcing it to everyone with bombastic conviction.

Hospitality

While Louis XIV may have devised his rules to prevent people from getting above their station, and to quash any potential revolution, in the hundreds of years since then, etiquette has evolved to include all people wherever possible. As we will see, the rules of table conversation evolved to ensure that the people on each side of you were spoken to equally during dinner, so that no one was excluded.

I promise I am not being sponsored by Visit Britain, but once again, we lead the way. Our hospitality is not merely by accident but by design – shaped by centuries of interaction, integration and influence from across the globe. The British Isles have always been a crossroads of civilisations, ideas and peoples, each leaving an indelible mark on the country's culture, cuisine and character – like the houseguest that leaves a mark on the herringbone wood block, but in these instances, a more palatable one.

Our education and legal frameworks further cement Britain's commitment to inclusivity, promoting equality and protecting the rights of all citizens, regardless of their background. The school curriculum today, for instance, is designed to foster an understanding and appreciation of different cultures, religions, sexualities, genders and ways of life, preparing each generation to value diversity and realise there are many other worlds outside our own.

Away from the whiteboards and exam halls, our global outlook and role as a nexus of the Commonwealth have fostered connections – though historically not always consensually – with countries and cultures around the world, enriching our own nation with a variety of perspectives and experiences.

Rank

Britain is not a new country, and therefore is one consumed by titles; many historic, others meaningless. Brits will usually defer to rank, even if less subserviently than our ancestors would. Even those who say they don't care about grand titles quickly adhere to them when put on the spot – face to face with the Vice-Chancellor of the County Palatine of Lancaster.

The fascination with rank and titles is emblematic of a society deeply rooted in a monarchical and aristocratic system that has, over centuries, evolved but never entirely faded. This enduring preoccupation serves as a testament to the nation's rich heritage and our unwavering commitment to preserving the legacy of our forebears. It is a realm where the subtle distinctions between a duke and a marquess, or the precise manner in which one addresses a knight or a baronet, are not merely trifles but essential threads in the fabric of British identity, marking us out from many other countries.

This fastidious attention to rank and titles underscores a broader cultural ethos that prizes respect, formality and the recognition of achievement and status. The column inches devoted to the issue of whether Harry and Meghan should be stripped of their titles would not have existed anywhere else, as no other country cares as much as the British; titles carry cachet, and are a way for us to respect the institutions and celebrate the achievements of those around us.

Many forget that when we bow or curtsy to the monarch, we are not genuflecting because that person is any better than us. We are acknowledging that they hold the most important office – and in this instance, we are respecting the office, not the person. Although we may well respect the person, too.

Patience

Queueing is a quintessentially British phenomenon, however hackneyed, that epitomises the key mannerly virtue of patience. Whether waiting for public transport, at the supermarket checkout or in receiving lines at weddings, Britons exhibit remarkable patience, respecting the principle of 'first come, first served'. Break that rule at your peril.

Moreover, British etiquette emphasises the importance of listening attentively and allowing others to express themselves fully before responding. You only have to compare debate segments on British and American television and radio to realise that, although not perfect, most British guests will wait for the other person to finish their point – however ludicrous – or get very annoyed if they themselves are cut off mid-flow. Thoughtful communication is valued over hasty, ill-conceived reactions.

Much of our dining etiquette and table manners are based on delayed gratification. The ritual of afternoon tea encourages participants to savour the moment and engage in unhurried conversation over several hours – the antidote to the ultra-processed, fast-food meal-deal culture of gobble and go.

Passive aggression

The penultimate key principle of British manners is passive aggression. It is a perfect way for Brits to avoid being be too direct, allowing us to hide behind some tart humour.

Our humble approach to including people, whatever their rank, and with our characteristic stoicism has led to a healthy helping of gentle insincerity. We know we are meant to be polite and always consider others, and generally always do, but often this manifests itself in slightly maniacal turns of phrase. As we will see throughout this book, a recurring theme is our passive-aggressive edge. We'll visit the courteous cathedral and discover the Bishop of Norwich later.

A popular graphic on the internet is the three-columned chart of 'What the British say, what the British mean, and what foreigners understand'. This, too, is laden with a good helping of the pass-ag. When Brits say 'With all due respect', we are not actually giving any respect beyond paying lip service to the notion. What we Brits actually mean is: 'You are a complete nit, but we understand, as humans in a civilised society, that we can't just say that.'

This passive aggression only really comes out in our manners when the other person fails to be as courteous as we strive to be. If everyone were as courteous and considerate as they are meant to be, we would not have to flex our pass-ag muscles.

Humour

Finally, a key value of British good manners is having a sense of humour. We may be fiercely protective, but we can laugh at ourselves and the etiquette we have created. There is a danger that those not acclimatised to Britain think we are taking it all deathly seriously. Often, we are not. We find our quirks and eccentricities most amusing.

Our funny bone is also a defence mechanism. The first reaction to something objectionable or bizarre is to find something funny rather than jumping straight to outrage. There is a widely held belief that the British sense of humour and our love of satire (of ourselves and our leaders) is the best protection against a dictator or despot taking power. We'd just laugh at them, quashing any power they thought they had.

The rules, however, will change and adapt over time. As we invent new technologies and become more aware of different perspectives, the etiquette and manners will evolve. Never assume we can cease learning what's correct and what isn't as certain things will become outdated. For those of us secure enough in our skin, that's more exciting than a freshly starched, crisp white napkin. Though the rules will vary, I suspect the six principles will remain as the six cornerstones of the hexagonal cathedral of British manners.

But while we believe that respect, tolerance, humility, inclusion, good humour and patience are all needed, and that no one is exempt from displaying common courtesy, we are aware that at times there are things of greater importance than whether the cream goes first or last on a scone.

CHAPTER TWO

How Do You Do

Brits are not known for effusive, tactile greetings, and probably never will be.

We generally like to leave all that to countries like Spain and Argentina, where it's much freer and looser than it is for us in Britain. A kiss here, an abrazo there – handing them out like free condoms at a GUM clinic. Far too much for our delicate sensibilities. While the dams in front of us Brits' tear ducts may have burst in August '97 when Diana, Princess of Wales, died, we're still more reserved than those in many other countries.

The traditional observation about us was that we only showed emotion to dogs and horses. This is no longer completely true, and showing emotion towards family and most friends is now positively encouraged and doesn't make you any less of a Brit than if you appear to treat them with disinterest.

But where our more reserved nature is still in play is when meeting strangers. Many of the international students in my etiquette classes over the years have commented that when they meet a trad

Brit, they often assume they are either being treated with suspicion or are not liked. Rarely do they seem to meet a Brit and feel like they have made a new best friend. This may well be a hangover from a more emotionless time, but for many it is actually a sign of their insecurity and social uncertainty. They simply don't quite know what to do or say, as no one has told them with any clarity.

Take handshakes, for example. A parent may tell their child how to shake hands when the latter is still in short trousers, but after that, no one says anything about it ever again, which is a bit unfair as our hands (and our strength) grow. There are rarely any further lessons on how to shake a hand. Unless you are like the resident tour de force at my school, Mrs Hallworth. One day in assembly, a sports team in the upper sixth (year 13) had won some competition and were invited to come to collect their medals from the headmaster and Mrs Hallworth, the deputy head. All a bit much for some gilded plastic tat, if you asked me. As the rugger lads waddled back down the chapel's nave to retake their seats, Mrs Hallworth pounced back in front of the microphone on the lectern and demanded they all come back. Their handshakes had all been weak and feeble, she said. They were to return and shake hands again, but with a firmer grip.

Mrs H was not a woman with whom you argued. Calling out their wet-fish shakes in front of 685 other pupils was a gutsy move, so my lips couldn't help but curl upwards into a smile at her audacity. They'll never shake hands badly again, I thought to myself.

A handshake's quality cannot be exclusively British. Each country has a preference for the number of pumps and firmness of the grip. Where we have added our own take on the standard greeting of a stranger is in what we say while shaking, and how that indicates which social class we are from.

While we love procedure and form, Brits are positively horizontal compared to the Japanese, perhaps the only nation whose etiquette and protocols make us look relaxed. An early client of The English Manner, way back before I worked for, let alone owned, the company, was the London office of an American law firm, who had flown over to Osaka to negotiate a multimillion-dollar deal on behalf of a client. At 9 a.m. on the first day, in processed their Japanese counterparts in their almost identical suits. The head of the Western delegation came around the boardroom table to start the greetings, but he extended his hand to the second in command at the host firm rather than their number one. (Granted, only as the second in command was closer in proximity.) Cue some just-about audible gasps before the Japanese lawyers turned around and left the boardroom. The negotiations had ended as quickly as they had begun.

Ironically, as is always the way, the American firm had rejected my colleague's approach to facilitate some etiquette training only a few weeks before the Osaka visit. Only once they got home, their heads hung in shame, did they realise they should have said yes to the etiquette training, and they soon got back in touch. We Brits may think that was a bit highly strung of the Japanese firm, even by our standards – but it is not our culture, it's theirs, and the Americans were on their territory. Although, I would posit that maybe the Japanese delegation was looking for an excuse to withdraw from the deal anyway.

Wherever you are in the world, how you greet someone or they greet you is key – as it is the first example of a person's manners, and you can tell much about a person within the first moments you spend with them.

Introducing yourself

Until relatively recently, introducing yourself to someone in a social setting was one of the rudest things you could do. It was bold, brash and distinctly not the done thing. You may as well have walked up to them and licked their face while giving your name. Similar works to the one you are reading now, but printed in a different decade, did not contain any advice on how to self-introduce. That's how taboo it was.

Even over in the more direct America, Emily Post's 1922 original *Etiquette in Society, in Business, in Politics, and at Home* made scant reference to this. Only if a man was not introduced by the hostess to the lady he was escorting into a dinner could he introduce himself.

Luckily for us all, on either side of the ocean, we can now introduce ourselves to other people without fear of being sent to social Siberia. It is always preferable, and more relaxing, to have someone vouch for you and do the introduction, but fewer people nowadays know how to do this – probably thanks to the scales tipping well in favour of self-introduction. But you must introduce yourself, or be introduced, in order to be accepted by Brits. Without an introduction of any kind, you will only half-exist socially.

My mother and I have a long-standing joke between us in which she refers to her friend Jane, who I once saw when I was collecting my mother from a tennis game she played with friends. I knew two of her friends very well but had never met Jane. Innocently forgetting this, my mother did not introduce me, and now anytime Jane is mentioned, she is 'Jane-who-I-didn't-introduce-you-to'. Years later, I am still to meet Jane.

It need not be any more complicated than 'Hello, I'm John Worthing' with an extension of the hand, or whatever other physical greeting you deem fit. (More on that soon.) For more formal settings, the 'hello' can be switched with 'good morning/afternoon/evening'. Unless you are in a nightclub or some other relaxed den of iniquity, it remains correct to give both your given and your family name. This helps people remember your name, and if you have one they have heard of before (for whatever reason), they will know you. There is a marked difference between how people will react to 'Hello, I'm Harry' and 'Hello, I'm Harry Potter'. The scar may be a bit of a giveaway, too, I guess.

If you are wearing headphones or earbuds, these should be removed completely when you introduce yourself, and should only be placed back in when you have parted. Similarly, sunglasses are best removed for introductions and initial conversation.

How do you do

If you are moving in trad-Brit circles, you may also hear 'How do you do' tagged onto an introduction to a stranger. This is an old way of asking 'How are you', but it still just about remains in top society, although it is definitely less prevalent and much less of a social marker than it once was. Its origins date back to 1611, to the Jacobean comic play by Thomas Middleton *No Wit, No Help Like a Woman's*. Before 'how do you do' became a thing, it was the shorter 'how do' to enquire, rhetorically, about someone's health.

For those new to the use of 'How do you do', note that it is a rhetorical question and asked as a statement with no rising inflection, unlike most interrogatives or the pattern of speech of the cast of *Neighbours*. It's not right to actually answer the question – harsh as it may sound, Brits don't really care about the immediate welfare of a stranger, as they have yet to build any connection with that person. The response to 'How do you do' is to repeat it exactly: 'How do you do.'

Younger generations, who are much more promiscuous with the class of contacts in their social circle than older generations, are less likely to use 'How do you do', however. Using it can lead to confusion in other countries, and communication is at its best when people can understand you. I believe that a good greeting today doesn't have to have it at all to make perfect sense. 'Good morning. John Worthing' is great. Should you wish to use it, of course – perhaps you're meeting a ennobled earl or a dusty dowager – you can add it before or after your name.

Previously, it was social game-over for anyone who greeted some-one with 'Pleased to meet you' or 'Nice to meet you'. While no one would have flinched, said anything out loud or tasered you, some Brits' class antennae would have registered this, and your card would have been marked. But this has changed. Even the now Prince of Wales, William, has been heard saying 'Pleased to meet you' and the like, when touring the provinces, revealing his brass plaques and cut-ting sateen ribbons. This is somewhat ironic for royal watchers, who either squealed with glee or winced in shame when the family of Catherine, the Princess of Wales, were – years ago – known socially as the 'Nice To Meet You Middletons', as they reportedly kept saying this to friends and relatives of Prince William.

The main argument for the Middletons, or anyone, not saying 'Nice/pleased to meet you' is that if you have never met them before, you do not yet know whether it *is* that nice. While you may think you are starting with optimism, you're actually starting your meeting with insincerity, and we can leave all that treacly nonsense to the Americans – who are all having nice days. The other case for not saying it, and instead saying 'How do you do', is that HDYD signifies you are one of the British elite: you know your way around a dining table and would never dream of wearing brown shoes with a suit in the city or a visible tie-clip.

Kate Fox, author of *Watching the English: The Hidden Rules of English Behaviour*, strongly advocates for the return of a more universal 'How do you do' – arguing, without much in the way of evidence or examples, that it would make life a lot easier for everyone. While I applaud her pluck and sentiment, it just isn't going to re-enter the mainstream anytime soon. Use it, by all means, when you are meeting someone you are sure will know how to react to it – or, if they use it first, use it back at them. But it's better left unsaid for everyone else.

Handshakes

If you can, a quality handshake will always be, I sincerely hope, the correct first greeting. A person's shoes and their shake can tell you all you need to know about them. It's the only skin-on-skin contact you will have with someone. Probably. Other nationalities may be space invaders and go in for something a little more tactile, but in the United Kingdom you always know where you are with a good handshake.

While handshaking was originally a sign of mistrust (way back when, two men would grasp hands or wrists to prove they were not about to draw their weapons at such close proximity), today not shaking hands is seen as a sign of shyness, standoffishness or being socially inept. And Brits will treat those with limp handshakes with suspicion.

Only in the Scouts do they use their left hand (as they say, it is closer to your heart, therefore a true sign of friendship); everyone else shakes with their right hand. Point your fingers, closed, diagonally towards the floor, offering the other person your purlicue. (In case you were wondering, your purlicue is the fleshy bit between your thumb and forefinger.) Brits pump once or twice, whereas in other countries the handshake lasts much longer and can be deeper. In Latin America, especially in religious settings, you can nearly have your arm yanked off in comparison, due to the much deeper and more enthusiastic pumps. There are shallower but sharper motions in China, and in the Middle East they have many shakes.

President Trump was a gift for those who study the art of the handshake; he rarely got it right, instead – consciously or unconsciously – meeting people with a bizarre menu of physical greetings that very few people had ever seen and that they would hope not to see again. The one time his handshake was normal was when he arrived at Buckingham Palace to meet Queen Elizabeth in 2019, although – try not to laugh – due to the angle of the photographer's lens, the photo makes it look like the two heads of state were fist-bumping. There may never be any record of a normal President Trump handshake.

Bill, this is Ben: Introducing other people

While most people are better at self-introduction today, we have forgotten how to introduce two people to each other. Many Brits make a meal out of it and start breathlessly saying names multiple times, and often in the incorrect order.

In the race to be less deferential, people have forgotten that when it comes to introducing people, we do need to pick one person's name to say first – thus giving them an inch or two of precedence over the second person. But how do we pick? Who do we pick? The taller person? The one who is standing a bit closer to us? The one we're sleeping with? No. Once the following rules of introduction are committed to memory, it's simple. In a social setting, we first work on age and give respect to older generations, so younger people are introduced to older people. 'Granny, may I introduce Annie?' The next criterion to look at, though this one is beginning to die a death, is gender. Traditionally, women are given the respect during introductions, and men are introduced to women: 'Miss Laetitia Prism, may I introduce Mr Algernon Moncrieff?'

Note that in both these examples you only have to say each name once. What a bore it would be to say, 'Miss Laetitia Prism, may I introduce Mr Algernon Moncrieff? Mr Algernon Moncrieff, may I introduce Miss Laetitia Prism?' That second time, with the name order switched, you have elevated the man and relegated the woman. As well as wasted your own time and theirs.

To reassure those already breaking into a cold sweat over this, rest assured that there will be many times during parties and assorted events when you cannot immediately work out who is more 'important' than whom. For example, maybe you're inches away from two men of a similar age. Or you have your spouse's great-aunt about to come Zimmer-frame to Zimmer-frame with your own great-aunt. Where the difference is not obvious, it often doesn't matter. Just pick someone. If you really want to be fair, use the alphabet. 'Great-Aunt Aida, may I introduce Great-Aunt Zelda?'

In business settings, age and gender are irrelevant, of course. There, the introductions are based purely on rank or business relationships. Lower ranks are introduced to higher ranks, and colleagues are introduced to clients.

For any setting, what is always appreciated is some context with the introduction. 'Ben, may I introduce Jordan? Ben's just flown in from Panama.' They then don't need to stare blankly at each other, struggling to find something to talk about, but can instead discuss Ben's riveting trip. If you can find a link between the two, even better. 'Ben's just flown in from Panama, and I believe your brother is about to holiday there, too, Jordan?'

Here are some other pointers when it comes to introductions:

- However you introduce one person, use the same style for the other. 'Miss Laetitia Prism, may I introduce Algernon' would be wrong. Imagine their names on a set of scales and ensure they are balanced.
- Married couples are introduced individually: 'May I introduce Mr Bucket and Mrs Bucket?'
- If you think two people may have met, you can drop the 'may I introduce' and just say their names: 'Laetitia Prism, Algernon Moncrieff.'
- When introducing anyone with a title, whether royal, aristocratic, political or diplomatic, the word 'introduce' is replaced with 'present': 'Your Excellency, may I present Mr Cecil Graham?'
- Introduce an individual to a group: 'Claire, this is Faye, Lisa, Ian and Lee.'
- Say all names clearly and slowly enough for people to register them, but not so slowly that they think you're being patronising.

Hello again: Re-introducing yourself

There comes a time when you meet someone in the street who you have tattooed on your mind but they have totally forgotten who you are, but – being British – they are too polite to be quite so direct and ask for a reminder. This can bruise egos, but it happens, so get used to it. It's (usually) not personal.

The best way to avoid it happening is to re-introduce yourself immediately, offering a reminder as to where you last met. 'Hello, I'm Artemis, we met last year at Ashley's party.' This ensures you or they are not embarrassed – and, in the event you have forgotten their name, too – they should proffer it when greeting you.

In the event that someone greets or re-introduces themselves to you and you do not remember the person or where you met, it is better manners to pretend you do, keep smiling, and move the conversation on to something you can both talk about with confidence. You should only need to ask them directly what their name is as a last resort. If you do that, say 'Please remind me of your name?' rather than 'I'm sorry, I've forgotten your name'. The former is much more palatable.

One kiss or two? Social kissing and hugs

Never kiss a Brit on the first meeting. This is a sure-fire way for you to annoy them. It's too much, too soon, leaving nowhere for you to go once a friendship develops. If you kiss them the first time you meet them, what on earth are you doing to them the second time you meet? Don't answer that.

Until we joined the EU in the 1970s, one kiss was all that people gave to those they knew, if at all. Two kisses seemed like far too much emotion. But once we started mixing in the European common market, two kisses (one on each cheek, beginning with the right cheek) quickly became the norm. While we may now – infamously – have left Europe, the two-kiss custom remains. If you still baulk at having to do two kisses as a Brit, be grateful you are not Dutch, where they do three kisses. It's like having a bath.

A regular social kiss in Britain involves no lips or silly sound effects. One cheek is pressed gently against the other, and that is that. If you aim for the lips, don't be surprised to find yourself kissing an ear on a swiftly swivelled head. A social kiss involving your lips on their cheeks is only for very close friends and should be used carefully and sparingly.

Though if I'm being honest, even with all this written down, most Brits – even those who espouse the benefits of etiquette – have no idea who to kiss when and how many times, as documented when in 2017 the then Prince of Wales and Duchess of Cornwall met the King and Queen of Spain. The key is confidence, and try not to become too awkward or giggle about it to mask any awkwardness.

Confidence is also your friend when wishing to stop a social kiss – perhaps because you feel you are not yet at that level with the other person. Confidently extend your hand while walking up to them, keeping your outstretched arm more or less locked. Don't get too close, either. If you get close enough to be in their more intimate personal space, they will naturally assume you are okay with a more familiar greeting.

Even though hugs date back to prehistoric times, as a way of sharing bodily warmth, exchanging scent and pheromones, and indicating kinship, British people don't go in for hugs like Americans do unless you are a close friend or relative.

Stand back! Contactless greetings

During the COVID-19 pandemic, contactless greetings became much more widespread. The two key ingredients for a successful contactless greeting are confidence and distance. It will be awkward if you're nervous – and although this is true for all social greetings, it is truer for these lesser-performed ones. If you get too close to someone, they will assume you will be giving them a handshake, a hug or a kiss. Stopping half a metre before you normally would is a silent social cue for all parties that you're in less tactile territory.

The namaskar, which some call the namaste, is where palms are placed together with fingers and thumbs pointing upwards, resting the thumbs on the sternum – which, for the tantrically minded amongst us, is where we find the heart chakra. While some religions don't find this appropriate, it's a fairly safe greeting we've borrowed from India that means 'I bow to the divine within you', which is rather nice.

The safest touchless greeting is the hand on heart. Like the namaskar, it gives our hands something to do during the meeting – the right hand rests flat on the left side of the chest. It's also far nicer and less ridiculous than either the elbow bump or the foot tap (briefly called the 'Wuhan touch', before the British coping mechanism of gentle mockery had to be retired as the pandemic got more serious).

But the use of contactless greetings is not restricted to just plagues and pandemics. A contactless greeting may be appropriate when a man meets a Muslim woman, for example, or if you think you have the start of a cold and don't wish to infect the gang by touching them. (Although, you could argue if you are that worried about spreading germs, stay at home.) And when greeting people who are differently abled and may not be able to greet you in the conventional way with a handshake, decent eye contact and touchless greeting are perfect.

They/them/their: Sharing personal pronouns

This is where certain people may put down this book. But please, hear me out. When the telephone was first invented in 1876, etiquette guides soon followed detailing how to use this new instrument – an instrument that many saw as unnecessary, superfluous and a passing fad. Indeed, telephone directories often had appendices on how to use the technology for those who were not familiar. In some ways, sharing your personal pronouns or asking people theirs is a telephone equivalent of the twenty-first century.

With a fall in less rigidly gendered dressing and a greater acceptance of personal freedom, it can be difficult to establish what someone's gender identity is or isn't just by sight – and in most cases, someone's gender identity isn't even relevant. Unless we're psychic or have been told in advance, we cannot know what someone's pronouns are by looking at them, so asking and correctly using their pronouns is one of the most basic ways to respect them. Indeed, while personal pronouns are not uniquely British, our growing acceptance of the different helpful uses of them is the latest instance in a long line of this country being better with the name and identity thing than most, even if some will have you believe it's a more recent 'fad'. In 1862, Parliament upheld the right of any English citizen to call themselves whatever they liked.

When the wrong personal pronoun is used to refer to someone, it can make them feel disrespected, invalidated, dismissed, alienated or dysphoric. And that's the height of bad manners.

Regardless of any 'political' issues surrounding gender identity, stating your own pronouns can help those who have names that are not conventionally thought of as 'belonging' to one particular gender – for example, Alex or Ashley. Not that long ago, it was not that unusual to see a female honorific listed in a person's email signature ('Ms', for example) to indicate which they would like used.

Currently, there is no singular way to list and share pronouns. Humans, however, are at an exciting time where we are learning and finding the most polite ways to navigate this topic. There is an increasing awareness of the need for and value of pronouns. Many businesses and organisations actively encourage people to state theirs, where possible. Pronouns are seen on LinkedIn pages, Instagram profiles, email signatures, name badges and business cards.

There is no legal obligation to state your pronouns anywhere; but just because someone does not have theirs publicly stated does not mean they do not care or support the logic behind sharing their pronouns. They could simply not have a preference or mind which pronouns someone uses, or they may not feel comfortable sharing them publicly. A person's gender identity may not be known to their family, so they may use different ones at work than they do at home.

Even if a person is confident and sure of their gender identity and that it matches the one they were assigned at birth (termed 'cisgender'), stating pronouns can provide subtle reassurance to those who are transgender, for example, that they are seen and acknowledged. It normalises making it part of everyday conversation, and doesn't require people who may use less common pronouns or who are often misgendered to be the ones who always have to bring up the topic.

If someone asks for your pronouns, or you are giving or listing your own, it is better to give all three derivations (he/him/his, they/them/theirs) rather than just two (he/him, they/them). If you do not feel able to ask, or a person has not shared their pronouns, it is always correct to use someone's name. (You can also use the singular 'they' – which, despite what some English language dropouts say, has been used in that way for hundreds of years.)

Should you use the incorrect pronouns by accident, the best approach is to amend your mistake, apologise and move on quickly. You can recover from misgendering someone, so long as you do not make a big deal out of it. If you do make it a bigger deal than it is, it will not help anyone. Should you need to apologise again to the person in question, do it privately when an opportune moment arises. 'I'm really sorry I used the wrong pronouns for you in that meeting earlier. I know you go by "she/her/hers", and I will ensure I get it right next time.'

The person who was misgendered should also not make a big deal of it either, if the mistake was accidental and contrition is shown. While understandable and a perfectly human reaction, getting outwardly cross and admonishing someone to such a degree will not help people think about pronouns with compassion in the future.

Acquaintances

One small trick that can make a huge difference when greeting other people is to stop moving. This is particularly useful when greeting those you see regularly but whom you are not friends with – but equally are not sworn enemies. Your local barista or the receptionist at work, for example.

Rather than breezily walking past them as you call out a good morning, as so many do, take the time to stop, make eye contact and offer your greeting. To use a contemporary term, make them 'feel seen'. Offering them six seconds of your day where you are static and waiting for them to reply as to how they are immediately increases their feelings towards you. You can bet that most people walk past them and don't bother to greet them properly, or at all.

And when you next go to them with a request, perhaps you will get a more favourable response? Taking the time to greet someone is a small courtesy that goes a long way, and as life gets busier, it is a beautiful and simple act of good manners.

CHAPTER THREE

Rather Wet, Isn't It?

The humidity's rising; the barometer's getting low – which, according to all sources, leads to forty-nine minutes of stimulating chat for two Brits. Let's be honest, weather chat is not the most exciting topic in the world. But those who arrive in Britain to live or for a holiday sometimes make the mistake of thinking that we really do care quite a lot about the weather, to the point where we have a pathological interest in what's about to greet us when we step outside.

Wrong. The weather is used as a safe subject for conversing with people. Often people we do not know or do not know well. Rarely will two good friends meet and launch into a diatribe about the pros and cons of the day's climate – unless they are delaying talking about something a bit awkward, in which case, all bets are off.

You can talk about the weather if you are six or sixty years old. If you are blind or fully sighted, you can talk about the weather. Whether you do or do not need a wheelchair, you can talk about the weather. Everyone can talk about it and have an opinion that will not greatly offend anyone else; avoiding upsetting other people unintentionally is a key attribute of British manners and drives our conversations.

If polite conversation was an Olympic sport, Team GB would trounce every other nation – perhaps closely followed by the Middle Eastern countries. 'Small talk' is what we call this innocuous and often inane technique to ensure we rub along nicely with people, treating them with a basic level of respect.

While those who live in the bigger British metropolises may think they live in New York City and ignore the people they pass on the streets, natives to Britain in quieter environs will, at least, acknowledge those they pass with a smile, maybe a verbal greeting, and if stuck together for anything longer than five seconds, a few lines of jovial small talk so as to not produce any awkwardness.

In fact, in the country a cheery 'Morning!' paired with a smile is de rigueur. To not give such a salutation to a passing acquaintance would make them fret you are up to no good, possibly knee-deep in some bucolic crime syndicate. Meanwhile, in London, breezily smiling and greeting people in the street would make them assume you were about to jump them. Context matters.

Greetings are an art form that must not be confused for genuine interest. We are only trying to put people at ease. Well-mannered folk can do this easily – although, like in much of life, it does require two to tango.

The other week, when I was welcoming participants to one of my etiquette courses, I moved forward to greet the first arrival. Olga surveyed the room with a slight scowl, as if to query where everyone else was. 'Don't panic! There are more coming shortly,' I said, thinking I was calming her as I took her coat.

'But I am not panicking,' she said abruptly. I short-circuited and left the room, purportedly to hang up the coat but also to press my hard-reset button. Olga had fallen into the trap of taking what I was saying at face value and attributing too much worth to it. I had only been making a relatively light-hearted aside to fill the void of what would otherwise have been total silence. British conversation is full of idioms and hyperbole, and clearly these were not a thing where Olga had grown up.

New speakers of English also get caught out by our slightly oxymoronic phrases. What a Brit will say is not necessarily what they mean exactly, and what a non-Brit understands is not always what the Brit said or meant. For example, 'That's not bad' is modest Brit speak for 'That's good', but a non-native speaker might hear the word 'bad' and assume we are disappointed. If we as Brits were actually disappointed, we would have said 'That's quite good' – which would lead the non-Brit to believe we were delighted.

British conversation is also, compared to that of other nations, richer with reminders of our long history, royal and aristocratic. Especially in London or the smarter parts of the English countryside, people may find themselves inches away from a prince or just a few metres from a marquess.

While since the dawn of 'Just call me Tony'*, the correct form of address is seen by some as a little bit of an anachronism, it is very much still a driver for some in conversation. Does it even matter what you call someone? The answer, as any scholar on the finer points of protocol will aver, is a resounding 'yes'. The rules are not

---

* During his first cabinet meeting as prime minister in May 1997, Tony Blair announced to his new cabinet, 'Just call me Tony', in theory ushering in a new casual era for the British government.

overly tricky to learn and, once mastered, help distinguish the socially adept from the chronically inept.

First words: Conversational openers

Kenneth Williams, the great comic actor and raconteur, would walk up to strangers at parties and use a line from a song to get the conversation flowing. His favourite was a Sinatra lyric: 'I like New York in June, how about you?'

While our Ken may have had the advantage of celebrity for his more unusual but perfectly pleasant bon mots to pay off, you can't argue that if you were asked that at a reception, you would be more inclined to want to chat with the person who asked it, rather than if they'd made a hackneyed comment about rain. Though Williams was also around in an era where song lyrics leant more toward starting a chit-chat. Can you imagine mincing up to someone today spouting lyrics from Lady Gaga and Ariana Grande's 'Rain On Me'?'

Brits have an unfortunate tendency to use self-deprecation and gentle complaint to converse with strangers. While we certainly don't want to be as overly positive about everything as a Californian, we should take a leaf from their book and ensure the first words we say to a newbie are upbeat at best and neutral at worst.

Think how you would react if someone ambled in your direction and began a conversation with 'The band's a bit loud, aren't they?' Now imagine the same person approaching you and opening with 'What a lively party!' You would respond differently to each conversation opener, the second being much easier to react favourably to.

While Brits love a good moan, this doesn't apply when socialising en masse at parties and events. Unless they know every soul present, no one really enjoys those larger soirees. But having an Eeyore approach is not helpful.

What you are trying to do with small talk is establish common ground. 'How do you know the host?' is unimaginative but works – allowing your interlocutor to (fingers crossed) provide some amusing or interesting anecdote that you can match. If the host line of questioning won't work, the common ground you definitely share is the room you are standing in. 'What a beautiful ceiling!' you could exclaim, gesturing upwards. 'Have you tried any of the canapés yet? Any recommendations?'

Conversational death

It is still social suicide to ask what someone does for work as the first question. If you are at some professional networking event, then fair enough – your career has taken you there. But at a non-work drinks party or dinner, a person's job is totally irrelevant as to why they are there. The host has not invited Michael as he's a whizz with a jackhammer, or Stephanie because she's good in between the spreadsheets. Everyone has been asked because the host likes them for who they are and believes they will add to the ambience of the evening. Perhaps I speak from personal experience. Hearing 'I'm an etiquette coach' usually makes people stand up straighter in abject terror or gives rise to a pregnant pause as they work out what question needs to come next.

While attitudes around discussing jobs outside of working hours have relaxed, it is still not good form to ask this as one of your first questions. Most find it boring, and others may want to not think about work outside of their work habitat. But if the other person asks you or boldly brings up their job first, then it's fair game.

The big five topics remain taboo for small talk: sex, politics, money, health and religion. For some, this rules out any other form of conversation. But don't get confused between small talk and big talk. Any of these can be used, sparingly, once the pre-requisite five minutes of gaiety have been completed.

Brits are also not ones to love self-centred people who make everything about them. The best-mannered people will always ask questions about other people, and then a follow-up question or two about whatever anecdote has just been offered. Indeed, my husband and I have a rule that anyone who talks solely about themselves without much interruption for longer than ten minutes is probably not worth bothering with beyond that first chat.

When asked a direct question about yourself, however, there is a fine line to tread when answering. A Brit will not want to appear boastful but will want to give an accurate answer. The late actor Michael Gambon told a story where he was once seated next to an American banker at a dinner in London. When Sir Michael replied that he was an actor, the businessman chimed in with 'Been in anything good?' Not wanting to blow his own trumpet, Sir Michael, who had just starred in the multi-award-winning *Gosford Park*, replied, 'This and that.' The American shrugged, turned to his other neighbour and ignored the legendary actor for the rest of the evening.

Returning to our obsession with the weather, as the Hungarian humourist George Mikes discovered, if someone disagrees with another's small-talk observation about the day's weather, you can be sure the conversation will get off to a frosty start. For example, 'Bitterly cold today, isn't it?' should be met with total agreement, which will bond the two people. Not 'I don't think it is – it's rather warm to me.' You may as well just turn around and walk away there and then.

Good habits for conversation

People have shorter attention spans these days, and that has given rise to many struggling to hold real-life conversations and maintain the eye contact required. We've all been at a party and found the person we think we're enjoying talking with glance over our shoulder a few too many times for comfort. To mask their ill manners, we have to toy with the nuts in our hands or take a sip of something stiff. 'Cocktail party eyes', as they are sometimes called, are never good unless someone walks up to chat with you, in which case you must introduce the new to the old.

Parties are fluid affairs, and speaking with one or two people for the whole event makes for a purgatorial evening. The old rule still applies: spend ten to fifteen minutes speaking to one person and then let them move on. While speaking with everyone present is impossible, this tactic ensures they will not report you to the Monopolies Commission once they get home. They also probably want to chat with a range of people and not just you.

While asking questions is not necessarily nosy, especially if they are the right questions, during conversation the goal is to focus on the other person. Good manners are all about other people, and a general rule of conversational correct form in Britain is that other people are more fascinating than you. Rather than immediately entering into a competition, thinking about what story you have to share that is similar to the one they're in the middle of telling, forget about you and instead think up some decent follow-up questions to show genuine interest. Listening is not the time to rehearse what you will say next. Periodically asking yourself 'When was the last time I asked a question?' is a good habit to get into. Your own achievements should be discovered almost as if by accident by other people, rather than you announcing them yourself.

We all have stories and anecdotes we rely on to garner a laugh from company; our partners or close friends may have heard these stories and be sick to the back teeth of them, but they should engage their best BAFTA-standard acting and pretend they have not heard them before, laughing on cue and helping add some sparkle. Cutting in with 'Oh, not this again' takes the wind out of the sails of the speaker, and conditions the minds of those who are yet to hear the story that it may not be as good as advertised. Let people have their moment, and they should let you have yours when you want to pull out an old favourite.

If you do know you have heard a story before, and it is just you and the other person in the conversation, the rule is that you have just a couple of seconds to stop the story before it gets going. Use enthusiastic (but slightly pass-ag) phrases such as 'Oh, I've always loved this story' along with a big smile. Try to let them down as gently as possible.

To speak like a trad Brit, you must also remember what you can and cannot get excited about. Although, as mentioned, we Brits are not quite as reserved as we used to be, we still moderate our excitement in public and invert the usual rules of enthusiasm. For example, if one has a baked potato (which is considered the upmarket term for a jacket potato, by the way), one can enthuse about it to death as if it were manna from heaven: 'My word! It was the most exquisite baked potato I have ever had – absolutely delicious.' Whereas we might monotonously intone, 'It's terribly boring, losing an arm.'

If you notice someone not being spoken to at a gathering, make every effort to include them in your conversation. If that means you and a friend walk up to them, so be it. No one likes being Billy No Mates – show empathy and bring them into the fold.

Entering a group

I do not, here, mean what you should say when your friend adds you to the inevitable WhatsApp group about a friend's stag or hen do. I'm talking about an IRL group chat. If you have been left stranded at an event by rude folk who have ignored my earlier advice, there's nothing for it but to insert yourself into a conversation that is already mid-flow. But don't attempt to do this with a closed group – ones where everyone is looking quite serious, with furrowed brows, and they are standing in a near-complete circle with no natural you-shaped space. An open group is what you need. This is where most of the group looks happier, as they are not yet discussing the burning issues of the day, and there will be a decent space between two people for you to fill.

If you know someone in the group, it's a lot easier to integrate and you can meet their eye and get them to introduce you. Job done. For groups of strangers, it is harder but not impossible. Resist, however, that very British trait of over-apologising. If you walk up to a group and your first words are 'Sorry to interrupt', then you will be labelled as an interrupter – as that is all they know about you. They are judging you very quickly – which, although not ideal, is both human nature and animal instinct.

It is better to exclaim something positive or neutral in order to stand a better chance of being accepted into the bosom of their exchange. 'Hello, may I join you?' is totally fine. No one will say no, even if they'd rather you didn't. And should they brazenly reject you, they weren't worth chatting to in the first place.

This old thing? Compliments

The British are not known for being comfortable with praise. Older generations may not even have heard any praise from their parents for their entire childhood, leading to a lifelong affliction when someone says something nice. Today, most parenting has gone totally the other way, with the child being canonised for brushing their teeth. When the child grows up and enters the workplace – where compliments and criticism are more balanced – they become anxious that every time they accept a calendar invitation, they aren't being rewarded with half a day off or a pay rise.

The only correct reply to a compliment is 'Thank you'. But many uneasy Brits will still mobilise their self-depreciation gene and say 'Oh, well, I didn't really do anything' or 'What – this old thing?' Replying with a reflex compliment is also incorrect: 'And what lovely brogues you also have, Steven.' Instead, should you wish to give Steven a plaudit for his footwear, leave it a bit before you do; it will carry more clout than a hurried response to whatever he said.

Objectionable comments and serial interrupters

Etiquette books from previous years have never touched much upon this topic, as, presumably, everyone was too well-mannered to make offensive comments in public. Maybe also because not everyone had an opinion on everything – whether objectionable or honourable. But in a society where everyone is seemingly an expert on all of life, guidance is needed on what to do when an eye-popping comment occurs.

As with complaining in a restaurant, Americans may be a lot better with this practice than their British cousins. But as we adjust to the new way of the world, many younger Brits are getting ballsier with calling people out – and so long as it's done with an element of charm and tact, there's nothing wrong with it. While two wrongs don't automatically make a right, sometimes fire has to be fought with fire.

People with awful views are not very likely to change them there and then, so don't try to give them their road-to-Damascus moment. You won't win. Instead, very calmly, ask them, 'Please could you repeat that?' Most people, unless you really are in parlance with a lunatic, will be forced to think about their words, and will probably start telling you what they said came out wrong, or that they didn't mean it to sound like it sounded. So long as they correct themselves, a well-mannered person does not need to labour the point any further. Though you may, of course, wish to end the conversation shortly after.

Similarly, events are now awash with people who don't like taking turns and letting people speak. Don't emulate some low-rent reality TV character and scream, 'Can you let me finish?' A better, more cutting, reply would be: 'When you interrupt me, I can't hear you.'

People may also ask questions that are too inquisitive and personal. They wrongly believe that by removing all the usual levels and gradual stages of bonding, cutting straight to asking a forward question, it will save time and produce better results. They are often totally misguided. For those who do pry too much, a tart retort is: 'Let's talk about that when I know you better.'

Call me Tony: The use of first names

Familiarity breeds contempt, as they say, and it is always preferable – no matter what the situation – to stick to using a person's title and surname (i.e. Mr Henderson) until further notice. However, politicians no longer want to be seen as our elected representatives but as our best friends. If invited to call them (or anyone else) by their first name, however much the thought upsets your stomach, you would be excused for going along with it for the sake of an easy life and in the fervent hope that they soon clear off.

In recent years, being seen to be 'cool' has become preferable to being correct. But traditional Brits will shun pretty much anything that is cool and stick to custom and courtesy, at least to begin with. When meeting the parents of your new partner, for example, it is still the done thing to begin calling them 'Mr and Mrs Percy' rather than 'Ralph and Jane'.

Until only a few decades ago, children, too, were instructed not to use their friend's parents' first names until invited when visiting a friend's house, sticking to the more formal 'Mr and Mrs Webster'. But modern familial arrangements, and parents often having different surnames, make it very difficult for the young to work out who is who and what they are called. Most children won't use any names at all, or may refer to an adult as 'Oscar and Lexie's mum'. Whatever and however they do it, teaching the child to always look directly into an adult's eyes when greeting them is more important than them having to worry too much about correct form.

In a customer-service environment, however, where staff wear name badges or have introduced themselves, it is a courtesy to use their names wherever possible. It's remarkable what a powerful effect this can have, so long as it is coupled with your own general affability.

Lording it up: Addressing people with titles

'How do you address a lord?' is a perennial question I get asked, and even after the runaway success of *Downton Abbey*, people still don't know. While life is much more egalitarian than in previous centuries, Brits still have a fascination with wanting to ensure they know how to properly address their 'social superiors'.

The British peerage is riddled with unspoken shibboleths to delineate between those who are in and those who are out. A protection mechanism built from a historic insecurity? Perhaps. But probably just a hangover from a time when peers were the landowners and the demi-monarchs of their own turf. If a peer was addressed as 'M'Lord', they knew who was speaking to them and their relationship. If a different person addressed them by their last name ('Grantham'), they knew they were talking to someone different.

Today, even though most peers of the realm are graduates of the 'call me Tony' school of thought, it is still better manners to use their title, to begin with, when chatting, making an introduction or referring to them in conversation. If they then invite you to use their given name, do so, although this only applies when speaking directly with them in their presence.

All peers and their wives are referred to in conversation as 'Lord Windermere' or 'Lady Windermere' – with the exception of dukes and duchesses, who are referred to plainly as 'Duke' and 'Duchess'. Yes, that may sound a bit odd ('Good morning, Duke'), but in the words of the Dowager Countess of Grantham in the aforementioned television series, 'If I were to ever search for logic, I wouldn't look for it among the English upper class.' 'Your Grace' is also fine for non-royal Dukes and Duchesses. Referring to a peer as 'the Earl of Erne' is a solecism. 'Lord Erne' is the correct form when introducing or naming them in conversation.

Finally on this subject, know that the lesser the title, the more people care about it. It is rare to find a duke who becomes cross when his first name is used erroneously. But a baron called Alan will be less than sweet if not afforded the absolutely correct title.

For those who do need a quick reminder as to the order for peers of the realm, the following table is in descending order of precedence.

Duke	Duchess
Marquess	Marchioness
Earl	Countess
Viscount	Viscountess
Baron	Baroness

Clang! Name-dropping

Unless completely relevant to the story, the mere mention of 'Lady Barlow' is somewhat of a name drop. Not only that, it may have the unwanted effect of distracting from the anecdote. While it is usually good manners to give the name of whichever friend you are talking about, the exception to the rule would be titled folk and major celebrities.

If you find yourself conversing with a serial name-dropper, the best approach is to ignore their attempts to gain social cachet, or – better still – name-drop an even shinier name back.

Terms of endearment, darling

These are often fun, but never appropriate in a business setting, unless you work in the 'meeja' or art world. Terms of endearment should be reserved for those for whom you actually have some genuine affection, and many Brits will attach one to a friend or relative's name. As with most areas of etiquette and correct form, there are preferred sobriquets you can employ when addressing someone. 'Old bean/fruit', 'dear boy/girl', 'darling', 'sweetie', or even 'sweetie darling' are acceptable. 'M'love', 'duckie', 'dearie', 'treacle' and 'mate' are generally unacceptable in polite society, unless used ironically. But do not use such terms when the endeared and you are speaking with other people. Then, just use their name. The same applies for any cutesy pet names you may have for your spouse. Not only are they jarring for Brits, but they may confuse other people who are not familiar – nor want to be.

Regardless of who is present, if someone asks you to stop calling them by whatever term of endearment you have used, then desist without demurral.

Breaking away

Those with gold-standard manners will never leave one person to stand on their own. Having no one to talk with at a party is a feeling worse than the flu, especially when everyone else seems to be having a gay old time.

It's far easier to leave a group of people (just wait for a lull in the conversation and say 'Please excuse me' and pull out). When it's just you and one other person, however, the best approach for breaking away depends on whether you are staying at the party or leaving. If you need someone else to talk to – perhaps this person is a total bore and you're struggling to stay awake – then it's ideal to introduce the bore to someone else. (You can worry about being accosted by that person for landing them with the bore another time.) 'Well, it's been wonderful talking about the evolution of the hole punch with you, Clive; I've just seen someone over there I must catch before they leave – have you met Jacob, however?' Then you bring Clive over to Jacob – who, conveniently, is standing nearby with no one to talk to. 'Clive, may I introduce Jacob? Jacob's just moved to the area, too.' And off you pop.

Gender-neutral language

Although you might not mean any harm, using language that assumes another person's gender (if that person has not shared their gender or the pronouns they use) can upset, as can using language that erases someone's gender by implying there are only two genders (or that only a specific gender is qualified to do a particular job).

Instead of 'Hello, sir' or 'Thank you, ma'am', or other language choices that make gender-based assumptions, you could simply say 'Good morning', 'Thank you very much' or 'How may I help?' And instead of calling upon or remarking about a particular 'man' or 'woman' (if they have not disclosed that identity), you could indicate 'the person who just spoke', 'the person with the raised hand at the back' or 'the person in the tiara'.

'Ladies and gentlemen', although often said out of old-fashioned habit, is best retired. In its place, addressing 'everyone', 'friends and colleagues' or 'distinguished guests' is more inclusive and mannerly.

You still can't say 'toilet'

Linguistics professor Alan S. C. Ross coined the terms 'U' and 'non-U' in 1954, and author Nancy Mitford popularised them with her 1956 book *Noblesse Oblige*. Ross opined that the British fell into one of two linguistic camps, and one's vocabulary revealed whether one was upper-class (U) or not upper-class (non-U).

'Lavatory/toilet' is the most well-known example and still more or less holds true all these years later, despite *Tatler* desperately trying to get some headlines in 2016 by announcing that 'toilet' is now acceptable. It isn't. But there has been some change since the 1950s. Ross and Mitford said that the English upper class would call a frozen scoop of dairy 'an ice' rather than the more common 'ice cream'. This no longer holds. Similarly, 'radio' was once a dirty word for the smarter 'wireless', as was 'mirror' when one meant 'looking glass'.

I was pleased in 2017 to be asked by BBC Radio 4 to update the list for modern life. I've tweaked it further, and what follows is a hybrid of words from Ross and Mitford that are still, for many Brits, social markers, and newer entries from life as we know it now.

U	Non-U
Antique/old	Vintage
Avocado	Avo
Basement	Lower ground
Carry-out/take-away	Deliveroo
Champagne	Bubbly
Cooked breakfast	Full English
Die	Pass away

U	Non-U
Film	Movie
(I'm) Finished	(I'm) Done
Hello	Hey
Historic house	Stately home
Jam	Preserve
Lavatory/loo	Toilet
Lunch (for the midday meal)	Dinner (for the midday meal)
Macaroni cheese	Mac and cheese
Mashed potatoes	Mash
May I have	Can I get
Napkin	Serviette
Pudding	Dessert/sweet
Pyjamas	PJs
Repartee	Banter
Riding	Horse riding
Sick	Vomit
Sitting/drawing room	Lounge/living room
Sofa	Settee/couch
Tea (sandwiches and cakes)	Afternoon tea
Taxi	Uber
Toasted sandwich	Toastie
University	Uni
What?	Pardon?
Wine	Vino

That said, some U speakers do use non-U words to be ironic, often with a slight Estuary accent. I shall allow you to debate the comedy merits of that yourselves.

It's easy to see how America and Australia have influenced English, as well as our more consumeristic nature. As a rule of thumb for correct 'British speak', avoid brand names, contractions, euphemisms and inaccurate words. Those last two are why many still insist on the china thing in the bathroom being called a 'lavatory', as your 'toilet' was traditionally your make-up, which is why you have a toiletries bag for cosmetics. A Georgian lady of middling social stature would have retired to 'adjust her toilette', which was her middle-class way of saying 'I'm going to the lavatory'. Upper-class Brits were and remain much keener on the spade-a-spade approach, which is why someone dies and a mother is pregnant, rather than passing away and being expectant.

Beyond lavatories, if the second-worst word has to be picked from that non-U column, it would be 'pardon' – both in the 1950s and today. Firstly, it's a contraction of 'I beg your pardon' (which is fine), and very suburban to upper-class ears, but mainly it is French-sounding – and historically a lot of the British upper class wanted to avoid this, which is why saying 'pardon' became so non-U. The bonkbuster novelist Jilly Cooper once overheard her young son say, 'Mummy says that "pardon" is a much worse word than fuck.'

But Brits, however elevated their background, are prone to mumbling, and you may well be tempted to ask them to repeat themselves. According to the Mitford-approved list, the correct interrogative is 'What?' We can improve upon this, softening it while still not using the dreaded P-word. 'Sorry?' is the better choice today when you don't hear something.

CHAPTER FOUR

Do You Know the Bishop of Norwich?

Until the end of the twentieth century, Britain was not known for its culinary skills. Our closest neighbours, the French, have called us *rosbifs* for centuries – purportedly as an insult, although the great British roast (especially beef), when cooked properly, is a joy for any culinary savant. Luckily for both Brits and visitors to our sceptred isle, the food scene is now much improved. Granted, we have purloined much of it from other nations, but you can tuck into food from all over the world in a very small square footage in most major cities in Britain, a feat only vaguely possible at the World Showcase at the EPCOT theme park in Florida.

Students of etiquette know there are three distinct styles of Western table manners. At the top of the tree is the British manner. This is the most formal but is also the lesser-spotted style. At the bottom is the American way. This is not meant as a slight on America; theirs is just the most informal – although, due to the size of the United States, it's the most prevalent. Lodged in between British and American table manners is the European style, which is a hybrid of the two. British table manners are distinct from European ones. This is not a Brexit thing, I hasten to add; these different dining philosophies have been around for quite some time.

As for why British table manners are so formal, that is unknown, although I'd posit that while we didn't have the culinary prowess that most of our continental neighbours had, what we could have was rules on how to eat the food that we did have access to. As George Mikes wrote, 'On the continent people have good food; in England people have good table manners.' Perhaps the fact that British food was fairly substandard meant that our ancestors had to develop techniques to slow themselves down, taking smaller mouthfuls so not as to draw too much attention to the variable quality of the meal.

The British class system, too, is probably to blame (or thank, depending on your view) for how we eat. The aristocracy did not work as we work today and thus had capacious windows of time to fill. The best way to demonstrate this, and the social change in Britain since the heyday of the upper classes, is to look at how we eat toast.

For a start, the shape of the toast is different. 'Posh' toast is often square and has the crusts removed in the kitchen. Middle class toast is triangular and 'common' toast is rectangular – both with crusts left intact.

When I worked on the film *Red, White & Royal Blue*, the props department and I nearly came to blows over the shape and style of the toast that we were giving Prince Henry to enjoy at Kensington Palace. Their initial offering was very bourgeois and did not meet with my approval. Their plea of 'Well, when we worked on *The Crown* this is how we did it' was met with an icy look. Thankfully, both the props master and the toast were soon cut down to size.

Not only is the shape of toast different depending on your position on the social ladder, but the way to consume it varies, too. The idle aristocracy of yesteryear would have broken a little chunk of toast off from their square slice, added butter and then marmalade (always thick-cut), eaten, and then repeated the sequence – with a swig or two of tea in between. Breakfast was never rushed as there wasn't much to do after it.

Today, in our time-poor nation, with parents trying to get children ready for school and checking the roads and rails for any commuting drama, the whole slice of toast is now layered all in one go, and eaten standing up, while rushing around the kitchen, or with one arm in the coat and one locking the door, toast clenched between their teeth.

All of this is not to say that British table manners must be used all over the world. Many of the rules of British dining that follow were codified based on a much less varied and less international menu. Spaghetti, for example, is not eaten with a knife and fork held in the British style. It's eaten just like it is in Italy, with the fork upturned in the dominant hand – no knife or spoon is involved. (Using a spoon to twirl spaghetti is an Americanism.)

Where possible, I have tried to reflect the sensible rise in the acceptance of left-handed people. Lefties from previous generations were not allowed to use their left hand to write, or to hold the table knife, or the like. Everything had to follow a right-hand bias, as the right hand was our sword-carrying hand and there were all sorts of aspersions made about those who openly used their left hand to write or cut food.

Rather than my colleagues at The English Manner and I saying 'the knife is held in the right hand and the fork in the left', where possible we try to say 'the knife is held in your dominant hand and the fork in the non-dominant one, but only swap when in action'. A tiny tweak to previously accepted norms that excluded people for quite silly reasons.

When I teach dining etiquette, while I do comment on the European and American way of doing things, I strongly advocate for learning the British style. As it is the most complex, it's best to learn that and then scale down to the other styles when needed rather than only knowing the American way and then embarrassing yourself when you don't know the more formal end of a tablecloth.

General procedure for private houses

While certain customs may differ depending on the style of the event, the menu, and the personal tastes and whims of the hosts, certain practices remain more or less the same for all forms of table entertainment.

In Regency Britain, if a footman wasn't to hand, a man would pull out the chair for the lady seated to his right. This was due to male-female-male-female seating and the fact that women of that era wore voluminous dresses and, frankly, wouldn't be able to get into their own seats easily without some form of assistance. Today, dresses are much reduced in circumference, and women do not need or necessarily want any form of assistance. Some older ladies, of course, may still be grateful for it. There should not be any fuss if a woman wants to pull the chair out for a man, or if a man wants to help another person of any gender into their seat.

Traditionally, men would wait for all the women to be seated before taking their own seats. If a woman left the table during the meal (which wasn't really the done thing but did happen occasionally), the men would have risen, with the man next to the leaving lady assisting with her chair. These rules can still be observed in more formal social situations if you are sure the women present will not mind – though most understandably won't want the fuss, and have come to loathe this bobbing up and down – but for business lunches and dinners, gender is irrelevant and instead lower ranks should hover until higher ranks have parked their posteriors. If someone leaves or returns to the table, anyone can stand up or give a half-rise, regardless of their gender. In fact, there is something refreshingly pleasant about seeing a woman rise for a man, or a man rise to acknowledge another man.

Once seated, resist the urge to wrap your feet around the legs of the chair or cross your legs, as you may when not seated at a dining table. Both feet should be on the floor and, for British dining, the hands rest in the lap when not in use. The habit of not putting elbows on the table harks back to medieval England, and is still just as verboten today.

The tables of our Tudor ancestors would have been makeshift trestle tables, made by placing a sheet of wood on top of benches. They did not eat sequentially, like we do now, but instead ate (more or less) buffet style, from food placed in the centre of the table. These platters would have been carefully distributed to help balance the table, which was not secure. If a muncher from the Middle Ages walloped their elbows on the edge of the table, it might cause the tabletop to lose balance and tip. Thus, it became good practice not to put your elbows on the table – a habit we still adhere to today as it looks so unsightly, even though we have more stable tables.

Dining is generally a communal ritual, and it is better manners to wait until everyone has been served before tucking in. The exception to this would be if the host insists you start – perhaps there are a few plates (often their own) left to bring out from the kitchen. But for cold courses, it is very easy for everyone to stay on amber until the whole group is ready.

The signal to begin is the host picking up their cutlery and starting to eat – or, in very elevated dining, this courtesy is extended to the guest of honour. Once the host or honoured guest begins, everyone else may. Again, the habit of male guests waiting until female ones have begun is more or less dead, with gender becoming more and more irrelevant.

A good host will start first but finish last. This is a skill that many are yet to master, but is one of the kindest manners a host can know. Good hosts will identify who is the slowest eater (growing up, this was always Granny) and keep pace with them – only putting their cutlery down into the finished position once Granny, or whoever else, has too. This ensures that the slower eater does not feel like they are holding up the table being the only person left chewing.

That said, all diners should try to keep pace with everyone else. This is harder to do when at a large table, but for smaller tables it is perfectly easy and adds to the collective harmony of the meal. If, however, you know you are a slow eater, make sure you reduce your conversation during each course and focus on the food. If you are a fast eater, pause more. For me, this realisation usually comes too late and I find myself having to dissect a solitary *petit pois* multiple times, all in the interests of good manners.

A key attribute of British – indeed most Western – table manners is a total absence of dining noises, minimising the awareness to others of eating all together; a sure-fire way to annoy any well-heeled Brit is to make noise when at table. This includes, but is not limited to, noise from cutlery scraping against the china plate, and the sound of frantic mastication. Your mouth should only be open when food is about to enter, or when you are chatting. Talking with your mouth full is grossly unacceptable, however informal or familial the occasion.

If salt and pepper are on the table, this means it is perfectly permissible to ask for them to be passed. Correctly, they are passed as a pair, even if just one is requested (remember that 'salt and pepper travel together'). If you cannot see them on the table, however, do not ask for them. This rule applies for anything while dining in a private house – if you can't see it, don't ask for it.

Traditional British tables will often be home to salt cellars, which are small silver pots with a teeny, tiny spoon – the salt actually sits in a slightly smaller blue glass dish inside the silver pot, as salt causes silver to corrode or 'pit'. Using the small spoon, salt is placed on the upper rim of the diner's plate in a neat pile. The tip of your knife takes a few grains of salt and adds them to the food loaded on the tines of your fork. This takes skill and practice but helps slow down the meal, which is generally better for conviviality and digestion.

While condiments may be passed, what is not passed is too much comment on the food. In previous centuries, saying anything was considered bad form – it showed you were not used to eating such good food. Today, it is highly likely your hosts have had a hand in the catering and will be seeking the immediate validation of their guests. You can exclaim with delight and admiration after a few mouthfuls, but in-depth conversation about the food should be limited. Guests can give a favourable review of the menu again in their thank-you letter or text.

Should you spot your spouse with some passata in the corner of the lips, or cavolo nero in their teeth, it is not good manners to tell them audibly in front of the rest of the table. But you do need to get word to them. Most people would rather know than not. Your friend here is eye contact and non-verbal communication. Lock eyes and, with your napkin, dab your mouth pointedly or move a finger towards your lips, and they should get the message.

I was once at a dinner with friends, and as we stood around their kitchen island having drinks, I noticed the host's flies were undone. Now, had I made eye contact with him and touched my own trousers, the evening could have gone in a different direction. Instead, noticing his Apple Watch, I visited the lavatory, messaged him that his flies were undone, and by the time I had come out of the loo the flies were fastened, and nothing more was said about it to this day.

British hosts are, however, prone to be overly self-deprecating about their own culinary skills. It is not unusual to hear sighs such as 'Oh, I've overdone the lamb' or 'My purple sprouting's gone limp' from the head of the table. This is not good form, and hosts need to curtail their self-critiques until everyone has left. Sadly, this has become more common thanks to the popular television show *Come Dine with Me*, where strangers gather to critique each other's dinner parties but are too focused on the food, forgetting general ambience and camaraderie – which are just as important, if not more. Unless something is raw or stinks to high heaven, guests probably haven't noticed what's wrong, so don't bring it up.

The British place setting

The British place setting has been lost. Thanks to the increased Americanisation of the Western world, what many restaurants and private houses now call a British place setting is, in fact, a bit Yankified. Even a purportedly stalwart British etiquette authority published a book a few years ago with an illustration showing a hybrid UK/US setting labelled as British. Etiquette land was – understandably so – up in arms, oyster forks aloft, ready for a fight.

While I am all for updating our codes of behaviour to reflect modern times, the table setting is where I baulk. My aversion is not founded in any sort of tableware xenophobia, however. It's purely that the British setting is the easiest one for all to learn and get their heads around.

Everyone's seen *Titanic* and knows the 'start on the outside and work inwards' rule – which gets tricky to explain if you start popping a fork and spoon above the plate for one course or, as some more bizarre American settings do, going totally out of the standard sequence with a teaspoon (for a pudding) in between a dinner knife and a soup spoon. Just why?

Having spent many years teaching table settings to people from all over the world, the 'start on the outside and work inwards' rule can lead to confusion. In America or in Europe, naturally, do as they do and lay the table their way. But in Britain, let's stick to what we're meant to be doing, as it's much more straightforward. Time to repatriate our tabletops.

Before we detail what constitutes a British place setting and what is a bit foreign, some general thoughts on setting the table. The point of a well-set table is to reassure diners that they will shortly be enjoying good food in good company. Those who arrive at a table laden with grubby cutlery, lacklustre glassware, and a tatty piece of absorbent kitchen roll in lieu of linen would be forgiven for feigning a sudden attack of the vapours and leaving, post-haste. Why have friends over for dinner if you can't be bothered to make them feel at ease, missing the basic principles of both good manners and hospitality? Make them feel special and like their presence isn't a total bore.

Even when using your second-best tableware and everyday cutlery, cleaning it properly and setting it out in a uniform manner can add a more upscale feel to even the most pedestrian of evenings. When guests first see your table, in an ideal world you want them to take a little stagger backwards, as they exclaim at the beauty of what has been laid in front of them and begin to salivate at the promise of what is to come.

When it comes to laying a table in the British style, the first rule is that cutlery is only placed either side of where the plate will go. See that space above the plate? Ignore it. Put a fork and spoon there and you have, in effect, deported the pudding cutlery. You can put it there, however, if you are doing a 'nursery' setting – reportedly done by nannies and governesses in children's nurseries to encourage the child to eat the savoury, as the sight of the pudding spoon and fork is a reminder that something sugary is to follow. But the nursery setting is really only acceptable for very relaxed dining, or if space is tight.* But before you finger any forks, see to the chairs. Space them out equally around the table and then start with everything else. Doing the setting first and then slotting in the chairs doesn't work. Save yourself the hassle.

While diners use cutlery starting from the outside and working their way inwards, often – but not always – in pairs, when you lay a table, set the cutlery from inside going outward. Trust me, it's easier that way, and helps you space them out equally. Another key rule – and this actually applies to all Western settings – is that there should never be more than nine pieces of cutlery in one setting. 'But what happens if we're doing a seven-course banquet?' I hear you plaintively cry. In that case, some of the required cutlery is brought out as and when it is required, often with the course in

---

* As will become clear, banquets at Buckingham Palace sometimes break the rules of British table settings for reasons of state theatre, more than anything else. There, the pudding cutlery is set above the plate, mainly to assist the footmen, who will crumb the table before the sugary course arrives. Guests are expected to draw their own cutlery down when it comes to eating the pudding.

question. Perhaps the teaspoon for the sorbet you inevitably need as a palate cleanser in between all that other food.

But, cutlery enthusiasts be tamed, the 'no more than nine' rule is a guideline, not a target. You shouldn't have nine pieces on the table if you don't need them. Only set what your diners will need. Even at Buckingham Palace, the cutlery for the fruit course at the very end of state banquets is brought out, finger bowls in tow, when that course is served – you won't see it on the table at the start. If you're not having soup, for example, there shouldn't be a soup spoon in sight. The menu informs which cutlery is laid.

As with royal entertaining at the Palace or even St George's Hall at Windsor, British tables are often straight-edged rectangular affairs, as opposed to the round ones now favoured in America since Jacqueline Kennedy introduced them for presidential hospitality. The linear shape of the table informs the accepted rules of our table settings. All cutlery is set aligned to the edge of the table, a centimetre or so away from the edge. On the off-chance you have mislaid your butler stick,* using your thumbnail as a guide will suffice. Forks are set to the left of the setting; knives and spoons are to the right. Now, this is where my argument of 'it's so much easier in Britain' may falter. There are exceptions to this rule. Smaller forks, like oyster forks and cake forks, go on the right; the

---

* A butler stick is a glorified ruler used by butlers and footmen to lay place settings on dining tables in a uniform fashion. It is usually 24–36 inches long but can be custom-made to any length (there is no universal standard). Some have measuring marks, and some are numbered with '0' at the centre of the butler stick and the numbers ascending upwards in one-inch increments each side. Thus, if a dinner knife is set at seven inches from the centre of the plate on the right, the partner dinner fork is set at seven inches from the centre of the plate on the left-hand side.

small knife for bread is now often found on the bread plate, which is set to the left of the larger forks.

The bread knife's position is a moveable feast. In traditional British settings, a small luncheon knife was set on the outermost of all the knives – the logic being that you used it first, to add butter to your bread (or, if you were being very smart, Melba toast). You would then leave it resting on the bread plate for the rest of the meal. Today, modern practice is to pre-set it on the bread plate, in line with the other cutlery, the blade of the knife pointing to the left, as it will end up there anyway. It's your call as to how old-fashioned you want to be. If space is tight, you probably want to be modern. Or, as a halfway house, do what royal tables do and have the bread knife on the table above the bread plate, blade facing towards the diner. Nobody really knows why they do that other than that they've always done it that way. A royal peculiar.

Wherever you stick your stuff, remember that in Britain all forks are set with their tines (the prongs) pointing upwards; knives with their blades pointing to the left; spoons with their bowls facing upward. Forks laid on the table with their tines facing downwards is a French and Italian custom – although, granted, we in Britain did also set forks like that until around 1750.

Bread plates are set to the left, aligned with the edge of the table. The napkin can sit folded in a neat, crisp rectangle on the bread plate, unless any origami has been practised on the linen, in which case the design faces the diner. For British state banquets, a Dutch bonnet fold is used – which, frankly, is one of the only ones that doesn't look highly naff. (Its name comes from the fact that the finished fold looks like the bonnet worn by Dutch women in the 1700s.) The Prince of Wales plume shape is also quite smart if done properly. Napkins in glasses were popular in the 1980s, and should stay there. Napkin rings are similar outcasts of the tableware world.

Glasses are added last (to reduce the likelihood of any breakages) and placed to the right of the setting, above the knives and spoons. As with cutlery, only set what glasses will be needed, and remember that no two kinds of drink are drunk from the exact same glass.

In a bygone era, there was a wine for each course. There may well still be today in more fortified houses, but most prefer to stick to one or two wines, and so there are fewer glasses on the table than there once were. This has led to the manufacturing of bigger glasses, as people want to drink a greater volume of one type of wine rather than smaller measures of different wines. A false economy?

How glassware is placed on the table can vary, but the general rule of thumb is similar to cutlery – order of use. The glass that is closest to the diner is used first; the glass furthest away is used last. How you arrange them is a matter of both taste and space. Some like a cluster, others a straight line. Your call.

The exception to the order-of-use rule for glassware is the water glass. In Britain, formally, we use another red wine glass (the largest-size wine glass) for water, rather than the water goblets that are popular elsewhere in the world. Whatever vessel for the water, it is placed to the left of the glasses, slightly detached from the rest of them, as it remains on the table for the duration of the dinner. Other glasses may – especially if the event is staffed – be removed once the corresponding course is finished.

In the Royal Household, the glassware is placed in a unique way that is not seen anywhere else other than at British state banquets. Six glasses are present on the table to begin with, four arranged in a square (white wine and water on the front row, red wine and Champagne behind) with a port glass ostracised at the very back. In front of all of these is a glass for the toasting

Champagne,* as, since the mid to late 1980s, toasts and speeches begin a state banquet. After the King and visiting head of state have spoken, the glasses for the toasting Champagne are removed but all other glasses are left on the table for the duration of the dinner. Royal occasion or not, coasters for glasses are never used on a dining table, no matter how precious your wood is.

Finally, the centre of the setting. This is where the food will go once served, but for British settings, nothing is in the centre when the diners arrive, save for a place mat or an OTT large napkin. America pioneered the charger (or lay plate) – this is a china plate an inch or two bigger than a regular dinner plate and used purely for decoration, but we're a little sceptical about them this side of the Atlantic.

While there are many images available online of the British state banquet table complete with silver gilt lay plates from the George IV Grand Service, it must be noted that such images were taken from a display for the summer opening of Buckingham Palace. In both 2008 and 2015 the Royal Collection Trust did an exhibition on state entertaining and – for whatever reason – decided to go the full whack and amaze the tourists with every bit of bling they could find. For actual state banquets, the Dutch bonnet napkin sits in the middle of the setting, but nothing else.

Do mind the overhang! Tablecloths and place mats

If your dining table has a surface only a mother could love, you probably want to cover it with a cloth. White is a timeless choice and always looks the smartest, but coloured ones are acceptable,

---

* Toasting Champagne is usually drier than the sweeter, demi-sec Champagne served to accompany the pudding.

with the inky exception of black. I used to think the latter were just some sort of sick joke you'd see on bad episodes of *Come Dine with Me*, but seemingly not. People do actually buy them.

Whatever colour, a baize mat underneath will protect the table – unless you really hate the table and are beyond caring. Tablecloths should hang equally around the table, with a generous amount of overhang on all sides. Cloths only need touch the floor when the dining table is being used for a buffet.

A more modern trend for table coverings is a runner – a strip of fabric that runs down the centre of the table from one end to the other. But while they may just about be acceptable for a swanky buffet table at a chic city pied-à-terre, they still remain high treason for any seated meal. They are most frequently seen at bridal or baby showers, making it look like some bubblegum-pink taffeta runway for the aeroplane of good taste fleeing the country.

If you are not going down the tablecloth (or runner) route and have a prettier table – perhaps something French-polished,* glass or marble – you will require place mats (but never mats and a table-cloth together). Place mats should be aligned with the edge of the table. In British houses, they typically show classic pastoral scenes, horses, ships, or scenes from Georgian Britain. In crustier private members' clubs, they are often just a block colour (a predictable dark navy or maroon) with a thin, dull-gold border and – if you are lucky – the club crest in the middle.

---

* The concept of the dining room emerged in the eighteenth century, along with the import of exotic hardwoods like mahogany. Whereas before this, using linen to cover oak or walnut tables (or simpler trestles) was seen as a status symbol, there was a new trend for polished hardwood from around the 1720s onwards, extending down to the English middle classes by the late century.

When Queen Elizabeth II visited 10 Downing Street in 2012, the cabinet of the time presented the then monarch with sixty bespoke mats showing images of Buckingham Palace – one for each year of her reign.

Cutlery

This is what other countries call silverware, but whatever you call it, it is essential for civilised dining.

The handle of the fork should rest in the fleshy part of the palm, with your thumb and fingers two, three and four wrapped around the handle, with your index finger going down the shaft of the fork, stopping just before the bridge. Forks are conventionally held in the left hand, which is why they are placed to the left of the setting. But when the rules were being codified, society did not think favourably of left-handed people. Today, we're much more accepting and welcome all of God's creatures, although tables still get set in the same way. If you are a leftie and eat accordingly, you pick up the cutlery you are about to use and switch for each course as needed.

Knives are conventionally held in the right hand – but again, if your dominant hand is your left one, do as described here but in that hand. As with the fork, your index finger extends down the shaft of the knife, stopping where the blade and the handle meet. Your thumb and other fingers wrap around the handle, with the handle itself resting in your palm.

Brits have applied their love of making everything about social class to cutlery, too. If you hold your knife like you are writing a letter, some snobs will label you 'HKLP' (Holds Knife Like Pen). You may as well say goodbye to any social advancement, shut up shop, and stay at home with your wall-to-wall carpets. Snobbery aside, holding the knife like a knife – not like a pen – gives you better purchase and control when cutting.

Spoons are held in your dominant hand, with the bowl facing upwards, your index finger and thumb sitting on top of the spoon, with your other fingers tucked into your palm.

Fish cutlery is held in exactly the same way as a regular knife and fork.* Yet again, however, we run into a class issue. It used to be that the mere presence of a fish knife on a table was a social marker that the host was a touch common – as fish cutlery was introduced in the late 1800s, and so if you had it, it showed that you'd had to buy your cutlery as opposed to inheriting it from your parents. (Quite what aristocratic adult children were meant to use while their parents were still alive and kicking, I do not know.) The canteen of cutlery at Buckingham Palace dates back to Georgian England, pre-fish cutlery, and so snobs would also argue that the Royal Family doesn't use such new-fangled cutlery, so why should we? Indeed, the Queen Mother used to eat fish with *two* regular forks, prizing the flakes of fish off the bone.

Today, nearly 150 years after fish cutlery was introduced, attitudes are more relaxed and fish knives and forks can add some decorative detail to a dining table without too much fear of social admonishment. Although the Royal Household still doesn't have any.

How we use our cutlery is different from our allies across the waters. In Europe, it is perfectly acceptable to turn the fork around

* Fish forks look more or less like regular forks, except for being slightly more decorative, sometimes with pinched-in sides. Fish knives look like fish tails, are blunt, and do not have the serrated edge of a normal knife. Their shape was conceived to help diners fillet the fish from the bones.

in the non-dominant hand, tines upwards, and push food onto the undercarriage of the fork before bringing it to the mouth. In Britain, that's the height of bad table manners. Not only does it look ugly (watch someone do it, or do it yourself and film it) but your elbow extends and, if sitting in close proximity to someone, you've invaded their personal space and possibly bruised them. Imagine sitting at a state banquet and doing that, and whacking the Princess Royal in the process. You wouldn't do that twice. What is correct on British shores is to keep the tines facing the plate, spearing everything onto said tines.

Over in America, if they aren't copying our style of eating, they are using a different method of eating altogether, dubbed 'zig-zag'. They cut up to four pieces of food at one time, then rest their knife on the upper rim of the plate, switching the fork to the dominant hand and eating the already cut pieces from the fork with the tines facing up. After eating those pieces, they switch the fork back to their non-dominant hand, tines now facing down again, before picking the knife back up from the plate. They then cut up to four more pieces before resting their knife again, switching the fork, and so on. Urgh. That's an aerobic exercise, frankly, and does not make for a relaxing dinner.

Even how we rest our cutlery reveals our nationality – actual or adopted. The British style is to rest your cutlery with the bridge of the fork over the blade of the knife. Historically this was to show you were not using the knife as a weapon – you were civilised, thank you very much, and would only attack before or after dinner.

When we have finished eating (and note, in Britain we do not say 'when we are done'), the cutlery is placed together on the plate, tines upwards, knife blade pointing in. People can get very fussy about at which angle this should be – really, all waiters and staff are looking for is the cutlery going together, but if you want to be super correct and British, place the cutlery in a 6.30 position, if you imagine the plate as a clock.

Glassware

You can get glasses for every possible type of drink now, especially wine. Websites boast the presence of glasses for Bordeaux, Cabernet Sauvignon, Grand Cru wines, Pinot Noir, Chardonnay, Shiraz, Riesling and more. Exhausting – and totally unnecessary.

While I am sure the shape of all these many glasses may improve the taste and aromas of each wine by 5 per cent, who has the money to buy all those – or the space to store them? That said, I do have an extensive collection of napkins for a man of my age, so perhaps I'm not one to talk.

On British tables you usually find red wine glasses, white wine glasses, Champagne glasses, and sherry and port glasses. Brandy balloons and liqueur glasses are also present but usually are found in the drawing room, away from the table.

Red wine glasses are always bigger in size than those for white wine, to allow more room for the tannins to 'breathe' and improve the flavour. Champagne saucers (or coupes) go in and out of fashion but are only correct for drinks receptions, not for dinners. Their wider, shallower shape often leads to the bubbles fizzling out a little too quickly, which is why the original flute design, which dates back to the 1660s, is preferred to help funnel the bubbles upwards and retain the fizz for longer. (Incidentally, the origins of Champagne coupes have nothing to do with royal bosoms, as some think.)

There is a newer trend for Champagne to be served in white wine glasses rather than flutes, as supposedly the more bulbous shape of the glass improves the bouquet of the sparkling wine. Brits are always wary of new trends, but as this is how the Ritz restaurant serves their Champagne, I suspect it's now perfectly acceptable.

All glasses, save for the brandy balloon, are held by the top of the stem. Holding a wine glass by the bowl not only transfers the heat from your mitts through the glass and into the liquid (affecting the desired temperature and taste), it makes you look like an alcoholic.

Sherry and port – staples of a traditional British dinner (and lunch, if you're lucky) – are served in much smaller glasses, as the higher alcohol and sugar content means you don't need much. 'Schooners' are only found in pubs, not in houses.

China

As a Duke of Bedford once proclaimed, 'Only dogs eat from bowls.' Advice you should heed when picking out your china. The smartest of British tables won't have any bowls, as pudding and dessert were only ever served on plates. A soup plate (a very shallow bowl with a normal-sized rim), yes, but no bowls.

A traditional dinner service will include:

- A dinner plate, between 10 and 10¾ inches, for the main course
- A lunch plate, around 9 inches, for the first course
- A soup plate and underplate, for soup
- A plate for pudding and cheese, around 8 inches
- A bread plate, around 6 inches
- An assortment of tureens and serving dishes
- A gravy boat and underplate

A square of chocolate. A square root. Sloane Square. We have plenty of perfectly lovely, acceptable squares already. Who on earth decided that we needed plates that are square? It's now almost impossible to eat in any purportedly high-end restaurant without being served something on a straight-edged plate, but to find a square plate in a private house is crushingly tragic and try-hard. But it happens.

Round plates are the past, present and future of correct dining, and take their shape, with the well in the middle, from trenchers of bread in the Middle Ages, which were used as plates. At the end of a dinner, it was acceptable to eat the gravy-soaked bread. This was the only time in history that bread and gravy was acceptable in polite society.

Napery

Back in 2015, the luxury duplex apartment with executive breakfast bar I was living in at the time caught fire. Thankfully, I was in the throes of hosting a small sherry reception for my lodger and a friend in the sitting room, as most twenty-five-year-olds would be doing of an evening.

While my friends started to do quite practical jobs, like shutting off the power and finding anything powdery to throw on the flames (it was an electrical fire in the boiler-cum-airing-cupboard), I bravely began to evacuate my assortment of antique napkins. Something which both the fire brigade and loss adjustor questioned in the coming few days. Thankfully, not a single napkin of any shape or size was charred, singed or incinerated.

Don't be fooled, it's not just a case of one napkin fits all. There are four different sizes of napkin. The general rule is, the bigger the meal, the larger the napkin.

In descending size order:

- Dinner napkins are between 22 and 26 square inches
- Luncheon napkins are between 18 and 21 square inches
- Tea napkins are around 12 square inches
- Cocktail napkins (often now paper, but you can get linen ones) are 6 square inches

In the grand, upstairs-downstairs houses of Britain, the theory was that ladies in voluminous evening dresses would need more protection and so dinner napkins were larger, whereas when perched on a sofa enjoying some tiny square sandwiches and a slither of cake, a smaller tea napkin would do nicely.

Today, most napkins readily available are a generic size, of around 20 inches. I guess that will have to do, and is always better than being given kitchen roll (always as an afterthought). Larger napkins are folded in half and placed on the lap with the crease facing the diner. Some international etiquette authorities get very bothered about which way the crease should go. It doesn't really matter. British manners are, in this instance, quite straightforward.

Whatever size your napkin, they are unfolded and placed on the lap in sync with your host, and do not go back on the table until you are finished eating and everyone leaves the table – leave them in a neat heap to the left of the place setting. If you are a houseguest, resist the urge to fold the napkin back into a neat shape. While you may be trying to show your host you can use that napkin again for breakfast, no decent British host would dream of providing any guest with a dirty napkin for a new meal.

Condiments and sauces

As mentioned earlier, salt and pepper may be present on the table –
it's really only in some higher-strung restaurants in France where
chefs take it personally if diners add seasoning, leading to their
absence.

All condiments of this variety are placed above the setting, either
to the left or directly above the space for the plate. A very British
condiment is mustard (English mustard, of course), which is presented in a small silver or silver-gilt pot, but with a lid across it as
the aroma can violently stimulate the nasal passages if the mustard
is left exposed.

Salt pots or cellars are always positioned in front of the pepper, as
pepper pots are taller. If setting a mustard pot as well, this goes to
the left of the salt, with the pepper sitting behind both.

At the head table for British state banquets, two types of pepper
are present: the front pot being for the usual fine, ground pepper;
and the one at the back a pepper mill for those who like it fresh.

As a reminder, if salt is to be added, taste the food first and then
add it in a neat pile to the edge of the plate. The tip of the blade of
the knife is then used to take a few granules of salt and add it to
whatever is on the fork, ready to eat. Not many countries still
observe this etiquette rule – indeed even in Britain this saline ceremony is fast dissolving – but it is still correct, and is the reason why
salt pots only have one hole, designed for pouring your pile. Pepper
pots have several holes, as pepper is cast over the food. Mustard is
added in a neat pile, too, on the edge of the plate, again using the
knife's tip to add it to the food. Things such as gravies, Hollandaise
sauce, tomato sauce, and whatever you've managed to drain out

of the Daddies bottle are delicately placed towards the bottom of the plate, inside the well. Although, those latter two should really only be seen at a barbecue.

Gravy (the English version of *jus*) is never poured from the gravy boat. Just because there's a spout doesn't mean to say it's correct to pour it. Re-citing Lady Grantham, British manners and logic are not often bedfellows. Correctly, gravy – and indeed all sauces – should be ladled onto the meat. (Please resist the temptation to drench your potatoes with gravy.) The ladle rests in the spout of the gravy boat.

The British way of eating things

British table manners are definitely more uptight, considered and controlled than those in many other Western countries – and definitely compared to many of those in the East. We have our own special way of eating what's on our plate, too.

Back in 2023, little did I know that an Instagram video I did on the British way of how to eat peas would metaphorically blow up, *petit pois* flying all over the place from the shock waves, with sixty million views and counting. In the method I outlined, which is the one I and many other Brits were taught growing up, the peas are speared on the tines of the fork, using the blade of the knife to help. As already noted, in British dining we don't turn the fork over, tines pointing up, when also using a knife.

One of the many incredulous and baffled Instagram commenters – most of whom clearly assumed that in the twenty-three-second video I was insisting that everyone must use this technique in all corners of the world or else they'll be cancelled – commented: 'This is a bit too English for my liking.' Others wondered why I couldn't just use a spoon.

The whole thing was hilarious to me, of course. What I didn't say in the video (because Instagram and TikTok are not meant to be used to communicate university-level nuanced information) is that in formal British dining, you aren't even going to be served peas, as peas are not a formal vegetable. Thus, the whole thing is a slightly moot point.

To those off to the Palace for a luncheon or dinner, do not panic. You are not going to be faced with a neat rickle of unshelled minted peas as you chat with the Princess of Wales. That is the stuff of etiquette nightmares (and the cover of this book)! You may possibly get some mangetout or sugar-snaps, but those are much easier to eat and are consumed in exactly the same way as anything else with a knife and fork.

Another big question I get asked is about rice. Again, rice is not considered a formal British food so you will probably only be eating it if you order it in a restaurant or choose to serve it in your own house. In the countries where rice originates, it is eaten in a totally different way – in India, often using a chapatti or roti to scoop it up, together with some curry, with no cutlery used whatsoever.

The British way of eating rice – when in Britain and arguably not when eating traditional Indian food, for example – would again be not to turn the fork over, tines upwards, but instead use some 'wet' solid food, loaded onto the fork, and then to stick the rice onto that. This technique prevents elbows from leaving our sides and jabbing the people on either side of us.

Passing food

For reasons I assume hark back to private service in our grand houses, Britain is the only country where food is passed to the left, in a clockwise direction. While some people know to pass the port to the left, this rule applies to literally anything you need to get to someone else at the dining table. All other countries pass things anti-clockwise.

In historic staffed houses, the principal guests (seated to the right-hand side of the host and hostess) would be served first, and then the respective footmen would move one place to the left to serve their master and his wife, before continuing on to the left to serve the other guests. Elsewhere, in countries where the concept of aristocracy was not as ingrained, the hosts were served last, and all other guests were given their vittles first. I like the latter approach. It seems a lot more egalitarian, although I feel unpatriotic for saying so. Frankly, I posit that not many Brits today know which direction is correct, yet alone that there is one, but so long as those each side of you are looked after before you serve yourself, the direction of travel of the gratin dauphinois is probably not overly important.

One of the tenets of good manners is the consideration of everyone else, but when it comes to the table, our individual greed often takes over and courtesy to others becomes starved. The politest of diners will always be looking to see what those around them need, especially in the first few moments of the food being served. Do they want any butter, for example? Has she seen there's sprouts? Has his water glass run dry?

Should someone near you not have noticed that you need something, it is the height of bad manners in Britain to directly ask for whatever you need to be passed. In all other countries, 'Stephanie, please may you pass the snow peas?' would be perfectly good manners. But for well-mannered people in Britain, the subtext to that is, in effect, 'Stephanie, you moron, you have been so incredibly rude to not see that I am sitting here completely surrounded by no snow peas. Stop being so self-centred and see to it I get those vegetables, post-haste.'

So, if a direct interrogative is off the table, what do you say instead? Passive aggression is your friend, and a lovely little dance of politesse should be performed between you and the miscreant.

'Stephanie, would you like any snow peas?' is how you begin.

'No, thank you,' Stephanie replies, reaching for the tureen. 'But would you like some snow peas?'

'Oh, yes, please! How kind, thank you.' And the snow peas get passed.

Not only have you not caused Stephanie to lose face at the table, but you have gone through the motions of showing you were putting Stephanie first and your needs last. Farcical as it may sound, it's a very effective way to get something passed without having to directly ask. Even if they just say 'No, thank you' and then nothing else, after a few seconds the penny really does drop and they soon then offer you what you need.

Tech at the table

Many years ago in Britain, people would say a small prayer, called a 'grace', before they ate the food. Now they take photographs. The custom may be different but, if I am being charitable, capturing your meal on your camera roll is the new way to acknowledge and be grateful for what you are about to eat. Formally, of course, it is not correct. And while it may be passable in a restaurant – again stretching the charity to its limits – it is the height of bad form to start snapping away in a private house.

Aside from any quick pre-prandial photos, nothing more techno-logically advanced than forks, knives and spoons should be seen at the table. Diagrams sometimes appear on social media showing that a mobile phone can be placed on the bread plate or just above it. The entire etiquette industry's blood pressure rises suddenly on such days. Jacket inside pockets and handbags remain the best and most comfortable places for phones when not in use, but as mobile phones have become a lot bigger, if you aren't wearing a jacket or don't have a bag it can be awkward. If you are seated on a ban-quette, you can place the phone on the seat as close to your leg as possible. If you are sitting on a normal dining chair, you can place it under your thigh, although it is wise to switch your phone to flight mode when in such close proximity to your lower body.

Asking waiting staff to take a group photo is a waste of everyone's time. No one in that photo is going to frame it as it won't be a good photo of anyone and the waiter will have to stand so far back to get everyone in, each person's head will be barely visible. Although, kudos to one waiter I overhead putting her customer in his place beautifully. Having taken a group photo for his table at the start of the lunch, after patiently hovering while they all found a configur-ation that worked, the table's host later complained, intolerantly, that the service had been really slow that afternoon.

She replied, with a broad smile, 'It's funny how so many diners think we are able to serve tables and get the food out punctually at the same time as stopping to take everyone's photos.'

The exception to having any tech at the table would be those dining alone, perhaps for business. As our telephones are now so much more than just that, it is forgivable for a solo diner to prop theirs up to read a news app while they tuck into the coq au vin in front of them. Although, caution is still advised – and if there is any doubt as to whether the lone eater would look conspicuous doing that, it probably means it's best not to. But for relaxed restaurants, knock yourself out.

Young children may be permitted a tablet at the table, in lieu of a colouring-in book, so long as headphones are worn and the tablets go away when the food arrives and do not come back out until everyone has finished and the plates have been cleared.

Full to bursting! Leaving food

No one likes a person who struggles to finish, and being at the dining table is no exception, especially when you have served yourself. Good manners require diners to help themselves to smaller portions if they aren't that ravenous. When being served by someone else, of course, it's harder to control portion size, so it is more forgivable to leave a little if you are absolutely stuffed to the gills.

Attitudes to leaving food have changed within the last hundred years. Before the Second World War, etiquette required diners – especially female ones – to leave a little of each course to show they were not gluttonous and that their hostess generously fed them. Then, with the war came food shortages and rationing. To leave any food was wasteful, and the rule was changed very quickly to everything must go. Those who lived through the war, like my grandparents, passed on this 'finish your plate' mentality to their children, most of whom passed it on to theirs.

Today, thankfully, with food in more plentiful supply, it is less taboo to leave food, but every attempt should be made to gobble as much as you can. Especially if it is food you have taken for yourself from communal dishes or from a buffet. The exception to this mannerly missive would be anything that is unintentionally raw or completely inedible. Please don't swallow any pink chicken just to be polite.

How you deal with being given it raw varies depends on where you are. In a commercial venue, you must immediately alert the waiter, although without too much fuss or noticeable commotion. Other diners may insist they wait for your replacement food to be served before they continue, but it is better if you insist they don't, especially if they're eating a hot course. In a private house, where everyone is likely eating the same, someone needs to quietly tell the host, who can then step in and extricate the plates. Everyone else should keep calm and carry on chatting, to help calm the now nervous host.

Do, however, note the difference between food you really can't eat and food that isn't completely to your taste. When being hosted, your own preferences and whims should be as repressed as possible for the sake of good manners. Eat as much as you possibly can, swallow and think of England.

There may come a point, however, where you really cannot go any further. Push the food you don't like to the side and finish off everything else. No good host will pass comment, although ones with fragile egos may ask as they clear, 'Was there something wrong with the rissoles?' This is where we revisit our old friend passive aggression. With a broad smile, remembering that rudeness may sometimes be fought with pass-ag assertiveness, you might retort, 'Thank you so much, I enjoyed what I had.' They will soon get the message.

A stiffener before dinner

Before you even move through to the dining room, a British dinner may begin with a selection of drinks, served in a reception room elsewhere in the house. Or, if eating out, guests may gather in a nearby bar to enjoy a stiffener before any sustenance.

Even if it is French in origin, a perfectly good and acceptable word for this custom is 'aperitif'. Sadly, many of the younger generations now refer to this as the 'pre-lash' or – brace yourself – 'prinks' (pre-drinks). These words simply will not do, so please resist using them, even ironically.

A traditional British selection of aperitifs would be red or white wine, Champagne and sherry. Gin and tonics and beer* may also be on offer for those who want a non-grape option. Cocktails before dinner are labour-intensive, and still, in some circles, considered suspicious due to their American origins; beer is fine for a barbecue.

In this day and age of increased abstinence and multiculturalism, there is no excuse not to have a decent selection of soft drinks in addition to water. Non-drinkers are sick of being fobbed off with the ubiquitous elderflower pressé, so avoid that. There are some excellent non-alcoholic spirits and wines that can be offered, so the non-drinkers do not feel like second-class citizens.

When dinner is announced, leave any glasses used for aperitifs on a nearby surface (even if unfinished) rather than bringing them to the dining room, like you are eating down the pub.

Puff after puff: Smoking and vaping

Attitudes have totally changed to smoking, and thanks to the Health Act of 2006, many of us are now conditioned to eat in smoke-free environments. It has become such an anathema in Britain that I was breathlessly stunned on a recent work trip to Dubai to see several tables around us nonchalantly puffing away as they ate.

* Beer is drunk from glasses. Only babies drink from bottles.

When a smoker visits a private house, they must ask the host where and when they can smoke. The answer will often be outside, through some French doors, and the host should provide an ashtray in the designated smoking zone. This stops hosts from finding rogue butts in the borders days later.

Cigarettes do now seem passé compared to the rise of the vape – everyone seems to be at the latter. While vapes are generally better for people than cigarettes, serial vapists need to exercise consideration when exhaling their clouds of vapour. Looking like the caterpillar from *Alice in Wonderland* is never a good look, however, so if you can try to reduce the puffs coming out your mouth, please do. Vaping in the bathroom is, like smoking, not on either. The rules for where to smoke cigarettes apply for vapes, too.

Cigars were once offered at the end of a meal to men only, once ladies had withdrawn, and the men would change into heavy velvet smoking jackets so the new attire absorbed all the unpleasant odour, rather than their regular coats, which they'd change back into when re-joining the ladies.

Port protocol

Although today the drinking of port may not be quite as popular as it once was, save for a few of the crustier Pall Mall private members' clubs, it is a perfect example of where Brits have made rules and regulations to add lustre and intrigue to an otherwise pleasant but unremarkable drink.

Port is a fortified wine, usually red, with an alcohol content of around 16–20 per cent and some fairly high sugar levels. Because of this, it is consumed in smaller stemmed glasses – as you don't need much of it. Indeed, historically, only the men drank it, once the hostess had risen and escorted all other women to a nearby drawing room to breathlessly talk about butterflies. Today, anyone can drink port if it is offered or ordered.

The decanter of port – often a wide-bottomed ship's decanter – is placed in front of the host, who fills the glass of the guest to their immediate right, then fills their own and passes it to the left. Each guest helps themselves in turn, passing again to the left. Some insist that the decanter should never stop moving around until it is empty. This is, frankly, irresponsible and should not be enforced. A more sensible approach is that once it has done a lap of the table, it rests in front of the host, who passes it around to the left again once they think it needs passing. There should be no obligation for anyone to have additional servings (or any in the first place) if they don't want to.

But what happens if the decanter stops halfway around the table? Re-enter the now-familiar passive-aggressive approach Brits have to good manners. Rather than directly asking for the port to be passed (with the pre-requisite 'please' tagged on), it has become customary to grandly ask the person, 'Do you know the Bishop of Norwich?' The decanter gets hastily passed if they know what you are talking about; if they don't, you follow up with: 'He was a lovely man but always forgot to pass the port.' Daggers!

It was reportedly Henry Bathurst, who held the Norwich See between 1805 and 1837, who gave birth to this pass-ag port-passing technique. Both his poor eyesight and penchant for falling asleep at the dining table led to his reputation of hogging the port.

Another method to get port in your glass, without having to cite deceased clergy, would be to pass your empty glass (to the left) to catch up with the decanter and then have the full glass passed back (again, to the left).

Port is never drunk before the loyal toast, however – although it can be used to make the loyal toast.

The loyal toast

Even our toasts have a rank and precedence in Britain. The loyal toast is a toast to the monarch. Other countries have this senior toast, sometimes to an office (the president, for example), and other times to the nation itself. If a series of toasts are to be made, the loyal toast should be made first. Today, this is simply the words 'The King' without any other preamble. The toast proposer says those words, and the rest of the guests then repeat them and take a sip. If there is a nearby orchestra, poised to strike up the national anthem, know not to raise glasses until after they have done one verse. (There's no need to sing along, it's not a football match.)

During the end of his speech at the state banquet for the United States of America in 2011, President Obama went to make a toast to Queen Elizabeth and said, 'Her Majesty, The Queen' (the first two words weren't needed). The band of the Blues and Royals began playing the anthem, but Obama kept speaking, reciting Shakespeare. All lovely, heartfelt words, but a total breach of protocol. In her 2020 book, the then White House chief of protocol, Capricia Penavic Marshall, gallantly admits she forgot to check Obama's speech. In order to be more well-mannered and take the bite out the sting, Queen Elizabeth broke protocol herself, too, by turning to Obama – once he had finished speaking – and saying, 'That's very kind, thank you,' The press headlines the next day read 'Burnt toast'.

Coffee, tea and digestifs

The custom used to be for everyone to repair to a drawing room and enjoy a small portion of coffee in a demitasse cup (which, for the benefit of demitasse dilettantes, is a very small vessel, similar in size to what we now use for espresso). But many now blanch at the idea of having caffeine so close to bedtime, so herbal infusions have relegated demitasse services to the back of provincial antiques shops – a great shame.

Alongside coffee or tea may well be liqueurs, although even fewer households now offer these. My very first alcoholic drink (aged twenty-three) was a crème de menthe frappé, which remains my favourite go-to digestif. Everyone should have one.

If offering an assortment of these, a smart and practical way to serve them – especially in the absence of staff – would be to have a salver of liqueur glasses, each with a different-coloured liqueur. The accompanying bottles can be behind the salver so people can work out which they'd like.

CHAPTER FIVE

Does Anyone Have Any Allergies?

There are arguably fewer things in life that give one a greater sense of pleasure than welcoming guests into one's house – except, perhaps, when they leave.

Many experienced hosts may not actually admit that the two parts of hosting they enjoy the most are the preparation and then the bit after the guests depart. That rather inconvenient bit in the middle where friends, and people you pretend are your friends, mill about your house, judging your décor and fingering your objets d'art, is very much a disappointment. The table you spent an hour setting, the rugs you got down on your hands and knees on in order to get rid of a stain from the last bash, and the guest loo you prepped and tweaked to within an inch of its life all get messed up, stained and soiled in a very short space of time.

But this must not deter first-time hosts or those to whom the very thought of having to starch a linen napkin sends shivers down their spine. Entertaining is an art. Like with painting or a musical instrument, it takes practice and tuning. Some have a natural flair and can make it look effortless; others slave away for days just to prepare the simplest of suppers.

Regardless of whether you enjoy having people round or not, it is the guests that are the priority. If you are enjoying your own party too much, then it probably means there is a guest somewhere looking for the lavatory, craving crostini or in need of rescuing from a tedious conversation.

Not just in Britain but globally, we have become much more relaxed with our approach to entertaining. The more formal, multi-course service à la russe extravaganzas are totally out of fashion in favour of 'family-style', where the host plonks the food in dishes down the middle of the table and all dig in. We have Mr Ottolenghi to thank for this trend, which will eventually fall out of fashion. While a lovely idea on paper, it's completely impractical unless you live in a sprawling Notting Hill pied-à-terre where you are lucky enough to be able to have a table wide and long enough to accommodate platters groaning under the weight of your za'atar-roasted chickpeas. Most people's dining tables are of a conventional width, and so suited to plated service.

And why bother even having guests round if you get them to serve themselves? You may have slaved away over a hot tagine cooking it – but, for me, hosting duties include serving the food, too.

However the food and drink are served, the principles of hospitality are timeless. Ingénues to the social circuit should remember not to run before they can crawl. Your culinary coming-out should not be a lavish buffet for all and sundry. Perhaps start with hosting a pot luck, where each guest is assigned to bring a dish or key item for the party. The virgin host still does most of the heavy lifting – making sure not everyone is bringing a lasagne, for example, and making the house nice enough to entertain – but the cooking is shared. Or, if not a pot luck, a small dinner for four, and then six, before you even contemplate doing a state banquet of your own. Similarly, do not entertain beyond your limits. If your table only seats six comfortably, don't try to squeeze in a seventh.

But entertaining is not just about hosting the party; successful social darlings are equally good guests as hosts. It is true that there is far smaller financial outlay when attending a party (except perhaps for buying a different pair of slingbacks). Yet there should not be any economy imposed on your wit, rapport and charm. Exemplary guests are few and far between, and if you learn the social skills needed, then you won't go far wrong.

A waggish American once questioned whether the Brits are any good at entertaining, on the grounds that 'there aren't any renowned hosts in Britain'. Clearly, this Yank had forgotten about hostess to the world for over seventy years, Queen Elizabeth II. Whereas in America the doyennes of the dinner table have either been fleeting or felons. For example, Jacqueline Kennedy – who, legend has it, once sacked a key member of staff over gingham tablecloths for a state banquet (quite right, too) – or Martha Stewart, great but greedy.

It is important to remember for those trying to penetrate their way into the candlelight-supper class that confidence is the key. No guest will enjoy being hosted by someone who is not fully confident in their abilities as a cook and a host. In this chapter, we shall ensure everyone is able to sparkle incandescently at their next soirée, and put paid to any rumours as to which country is better at the subtle art of hosting.

Drinks and cocktail parties

These are staples of British entertaining, and a good way to see a social circle all in one relatively short go (they often last two to three hours), although they are not ideal if you want quality time with each guest – and must never be hosted to pay off any social debt (where you owe return hospitality for those who have had you round for dinner).

Don't fall into the trap of packing your room with so many people you end up playing a game of sardines by default. Similarly, any music being played should start off louder while there are fewer guests – to give some ambience and mask any slightly awkward small talk – and then be turned down to barely distinguishable once more people arrive. I have said it before and I'll say it again: the best soundtrack to any party is the sound of people laughing, chatting and enjoying themselves. So don't get too het up about the perfect playlist.

Hosts of these forms of entertainments are well-advised to put away any terribly expensive or fragile ornaments. It only takes one guest who's had a few too many Dubonnets to knock over the Royal Doulton heirloom and there are tears before bedtime. Coffee, console and end tables should be pretty clear, so guests have surfaces to put their drinks on while chatting. Think carefully, too, about potential trip hazards such as footstools, baskets and errant husbands.

These standing affairs are not meant as meal substitutes, so don't panic about providing a lot of food. Ramekins of crisps, nuts or some canapés (we don't say 'hors d'oeuvres' in Britain) will do. The catering industry guide is to allow 10–12 canapés per person – which may seem generous when planning, but on the night will be gobbled quicker than anything else. You don't want people to think you're stingy, and if you can't produce such a quantity of canapés, rethink your approach to entertaining and go smaller-scale.

While you don't have to lay on too much food at such events, you do need to make sure your well doesn't run dry. Drink is the order of the day, and lots of it. Allow at least half a bottle of wine per person. For those who insist on watching the pennies, buy boxes or cases on a sale-or-return basis if you can.

The major difference between a drinks and a cocktail party is that cocktails are served at the latter. Sounds simple enough, but how many of us have attended what was billed as a cocktail party only to arrive and not even get a whiff of a Fuzzy Navel, let alone taste of a Dirty Shirley?

A cocktail officially has three or more ingredients – but be careful, cocktails themselves can be something of a social booby-trap. Done properly, they can be elegant and sophisticated; done badly, there is almost nothing tackier.

Cocktails were seen with some social suspicion when they arrived in Britain in the 1920s from the United States – as did most things that came to these shores from that part of the world. Younger, more affluent Brits had acquired a taste for them when travelling on the transatlantic ocean liners, and Harry Craddock's American Bar at The Savoy made them more readily available in London.

As a general rule, you can quickly tell the virtue of a cocktail by its name and colour. Classic cocktails will have simple names such as Martini or Manhattan and are roughly the same hue as their main spirit. By contrast, the downmarket Sex on the Beach shares its hideous name with a synthetic pink colour that makes it appear as gaudy as the person consuming it. Expect the ground to open up and swallow you whole if you give a Screaming Orgasm to the local rector.

On no account should you mass-produce cocktails in a 'pitcher'. Just because your local Sky Sports-showing pub does it, doesn't make it acceptable. If you want to make a large quantity of one drink, serve a punch instead, in an elegant punch bowl. Neither is it considered smart to have a bar installed in one's house. A corner drinks cabinet, a drinks trolley, maybe even a silver salver with a few choice decanters on it, but never a bar. *Quelle horreur!*

A drinks party is easier to do unless you are a skilled mixologist or have one to hand. Serve white and red wine, Champagne (or a sparkling substitute), beer or similar, and a choice of more exciting soft drinks.

Non-drinkers

Life is very different today, and younger generations do not, largely, have the same attitudes to alcohol as older generations. For me, this is encapsulated by my marvellous parents. When we visit, I will often ask the room, mid-afternoon, 'Would anyone like a drink?' To which I usually get the reply, 'Oh, it's a bit early for that, darling.' What I meant was a tea, coffee, soft drink or whatever. I did not mean I was about to come around with the drinks trolley.

If someone asks for a non-alcoholic drink – at whatever time of day – it is now the height of bad manners to question this, or ask again to see if they change their mind. (If they do, they'll let you know without any prompting.) The person may be choosing not to drink for any number of reasons – religion, pregnancy, medical instruction, they're driving, or personal choice. It does not need to stand up to the host's or other guests' line of questioning.

While it is bad manners to pressure anyone to drink or query their choices, people will still do it. Non-drinkers may be better placed to ask for something that looks like an alcoholic drink, for want of an easy life. Sparkling or tonic water with ice and a slice of lime is always a good one.

The man on your right hand: Seating plans

If you are not opting for a standing affair, your guests will be seated – ideally on chairs, of course, unless you've gone a bit *W1A* and are opting for bean bags. Plans for any seated lunch or dinner are incomplete without some thought towards where people will sit. I always enjoy putting people in their place, which can often make or break a candlelight supper.

For such a small land mass, Britain is awash with people with fancy titles – royalty, the peerage, clergy, diplomats and politicians – and if you are hosting any of these sorts, careful attention should be paid to who sits where in relation to their place in the order of pre-cedence. But today, for most people, the guest list will be non-entities. And that's said with love. Rather than worrying about where to slot in the bishop in relation to the actress, hosts should look at the personalities of the guests rather than their ranks.

If you seat the shrinking violets too close to each other, you can be sure of a conversational vacuum in that part of the table. Similarly, if you seat the bombastic extroverts together, you can be sure those around them will have headaches by the time they finish the main course.

Guests of honour (or, if there are none, then the eldest guests) are usually seated on the right-hand side of the host and co-host. This honorary position evolved from the days of jousting and medieval sword-carrying. A knight would always put the one he wished to protect on his right-hand side, so if anyone attacked, he could draw his sword (from his left hip) and protect them.

Know that there are two main ways to arrange hosts and guests: English and French style. But you can do either style in either country; they are just terms. The French style, reportedly popularised by the vain and insecure Louis XIV, is where the host and co-host are seated in the middle along the wider sides of the table. During the reign of Queen Elizabeth II, state banquets at Windsor Castle used this seating style. English style is often used for smaller affairs (Windsor banquets are usually for a cosy 156 people), and is where the host and co-host are seated at each 'head' of the table.

A totally different seating style is used for state banquets at Buckingham Palace, just to confuse everyone. The U-shaped table layout was first used in the court of Henry VIII. Not liking to change anything too quickly, it's still working for the Royal Household today.

A quirk of British seating that those in other countries, especially in Asia, find baffling is that long-term couples are not seated beside each other. While they should not be seated at opposite ends of the table, the thinking behind this practice is that they may be grateful for some conversational stimulation from someone they don't live with for an evening. In Prince Harry's memoir, *Spare*, he vents that 'Willy and Kate' switched place cards at their wedding reception, as clearly the older brother and his wife did not like that the 'American tradition' had been followed and not the British. (For what it's worth, while you could question the logic of a supposed American tradition being followed when the event was in Britain and a large majority of the guests were British, it is very poor form to switch place cards without permission from the hosts, whoever you are. But also, in American etiquette, you still seat married couples apart.)

Those who have recently begun a relationship with each other can be seated next to each other, however, unless they each know lots of people at the event, but they should remember it is just not the done thing in Britain to cling to each other, pawing at one another over their cock-a-leekie.

While entertaining on a grand scale requires place cards and perhaps even a seating chart at the entrance to the dining room, more relaxed entertaining need not have such a formal approach. But it is still helpful for good hosts to have an idea as to where people should sit. Brits especially will not move when faced with a choice of free seats. Instead, they will hover, not wanting to sit where anyone else is meant to sit. Hosts should not be afraid of being demonstrative and placing a few select guests, and then instructing the remainder to fill in the gaps.

A more modern practice is to write the name of the guest on both sides of the place card. Where the dining table is narrow, and thus the conversation is not restricted to the people on either side of you, this is an innovation to be applauded and very helpful for when you need their name. Place cards are always handwritten in a good ink pen, ideally black, and never typed. You do not set place cards for the hosts as it's their own house, everyone knows who they are, and the host seats, as discussed, are clearly defined. For guests, it remains the poorest form to fiddle with the seating plan. If you don't like who you are seated next to, tough. Hopefully, you like the person on the other side.

In Europe, they are partial to something called a *changement* (the French word for 'change'). This is where, often before the pudding, a second seating plan is implemented with some, or all, of the guests moving places – or even tables. At a state level, during the dinner in France given to mark the first visit of King Charles III and Queen Camilla, Brigitte Macron rotated the celebrity guest on her right, enjoying both Mick Jagger and Hugh Grant. We are often made to do it when I teach in Europe, but the guests over there seem to love it, while any British guests (including me) die a little bit inside at the trauma of having to start from conversational scratch.

That said, in defence of the *changement*, if you don't like who you are seated next to, it is a blessing. If you do like your dinner company, it is a curse.

Breakfast, lunch, dinner and supper

Those north of Birmingham will need to be heavily sedated – and there really is no argument here – but the correct names for the three main meals of the day are breakfast, lunch and dinner. Wearers of flat caps and owners of whippets will insist that I should have said 'breakfast, dinner, tea', but I am afraid I am right and they are wrong and that's all there is to it.

Of course, like pretty much everything in Britain, it's all to do with social class.

A traditional English breakfast involves hot eggs and bacon, but sausages or black pudding are often found. A Scottish breakfast is similar but may have Lorne sausage, tattie scones and haggis present too. An Irish breakfast (called an Ulster fry in Northern Ireland) may have white pudding instead of or as well as black pudding.

When working in Oman with Jean Paul, my Dutch colleague, we both looked at each other's breakfast with disgust and concern for each other's arteries. He viewed my eggs and greasy (turkey) bacon as a coronary on a plate, whereas I was eyeing his selection of cold cuts of meat, bread and thick processed cheese as a cardiac event waiting to happen.

A custom that disappeared with the evolution of gender roles is that married upper-class British women would have enjoyed a leisurely breakfast in bed, on a footed tray; unmarried ladies joined the gentlemen downstairs. Presumably, as they had yet to find a future husband, they still had a purpose in life and reason to rush downstairs, whereas a married woman, especially one who had produced children, could take it easy.

What remains from that tradition, however, is the rule that an Englishman is never served at breakfast, even if they are lucky enough to have a fully staffed house. The breakfast items are presented on a sideboard or down the middle of the dining table, and everyone helps themselves. Whoever is gathered for breakfast, in more traditional private households do not expect to enjoy an animated conversation. There is usually a relative, restrained silence while people adjust to the daytime.

While all British classes are in agreement on what to call the first meal of the day, after breakfast is when there's trouble at mill; people have gone to war over less. Today, lunch (formally 'luncheon') is the meal usually enjoyed between twelve and two; dinner is the evening meal. This wasn't always the case, I admit. Dinner was the main meal and was eaten much earlier in the day than it is now. But since around the seventeenth century, dinner has been used to signify the evening meal, for many often the largest meal of the day.

Tea, a term northerners use instead of dinner, is actually a selection of small sandwiches and cakes, enjoyed around four or five o'clock. The word 'afternoon' was prefixed to 'tea' by hotels to differentiate it from dinner for northern folk. Years ago, saying 'afternoon tea' was seen as a bit common and most definitely non-U. Today, the term is only acceptable in the right context. Hotels and restaurants serve afternoon tea, private houses serve tea; the former being much more glutinous affairs. Use the correct term in the correct context and you'll be fine.

'Supper' is a term that now refers to something different than it used to. Up until roughly the Second World War, supper was taken late at night – often several hours after dinner, perhaps having enjoyed a night at the opera. It was a small snack eaten to tide the diner over until the next morning – cheese on toast, perhaps. Today, supper is an informal dinner. If a British friend invites someone over for supper, then the guest should expect a *soirée intime*, round the kitchen table with only the second-best napery on laps, as everyone tucks into a lasagne or cottage pie. Whereas an invitation to dinner promises something slightly grander and longer in duration.

The British roast

For many, what could be more British than a roast dinner? A slice of a roasted meat, together with an assortment of vegetables, is classic British fare and definitely carries more culinary élan than fish and chips. But even this staple of a Brit's diet does not escape the rules of good manners and taste. So gird your tenderloins and prepare to carve away at gastronomic insecurities.

First, continuing the theme of earlier, let's get the name right. The generic term is 'roast meal'. If you're having it between twelve and two o'clock, you may call it a 'roast lunch' (luncheon, if you want to be really proper). If you're having it after seven in the evening, you must call it a 'roast dinner'. A more modern approach for many Brits, especially those in the middle-class bracket, is to have it in the middle of the afternoon. For whatever reason. As with weekday mealtimes, calling the midday meal 'dinner' is grossly incorrect and leads to widespread bewilderment amongst those who stick to the conventional mealtime monikers.

The items on your plate should be called by their proper name, too. Vegetables, potatoes and Yorkshire pudding should be named in full, not 'veggies', 'roasties' and 'Yorkshires'. Collectively, they are never to be referred to as 'trimmings'. We are not a carvery. 'The traditional accompaniments' is fine, however.

The more usual choices for the meat are beef, pork and chicken, although traditionalists may turn their parson's nose up at chicken, as it used not to be seen as very exciting. A turkey is fine for Christmas and sometimes at Easter. Lamb is fine too, although one British earl was known to not ever serve roast lamb as he didn't like cold mutton (who does?) when eating the leftover cold cuts the day after.

We now enter controversial territory. Yorkshire puddings are a staple when having roast beef, but only roast beef. They are not to be served with chicken, pork, lamb or indeed anything that isn't beef, as has sadly become the common custom. Friends who order them in restaurants to go alongside the incorrect meat are to be treated with extreme caution. Yorkshire puddings must, of course, be homemade on the grounds of taste (in both senses of the word). Bought ones are not the same. They are also so easy to produce you really do have to be cosmically lazy not to make your own.

Gravy is where many become unstuck. Remember, gravy is always ladled and never poured, even if the gravy boat has a spout. That is for the ladle to rest. The gravy is ladled over the meat and nowhere else. If your hand *accidentally* slips a bit, however, and some of it splashes onto the Yorkshire pudding, oh well.

A word now on the viscosity of gravy. It should not be too thick. You want a fairly light, but not watery, gravy. In fact, there is a saying amongst the snobbier end of the haute cuisine haute monde: 'Too thick, too council.'

Carveries and lesser hotels have developed the canny habit of feeding their diners more than one type of potato because a) they are cheap and b) they fill everyone up nicely, meaning they don't eat as much of everything else. But there is only one type of potato to have with this meal – the roasted potato. In a domestic setting, a proclivity of potatoes on the plate is a clear sign that you may be a regular at one of the aforementioned carveries. After being known to own a hot tub, this is the second-most damning social accusation that can be levelled.

As with the clear edict over the potatoes, there really should never be more than two kinds of vegetables (excluding potatoes), or three on a very special occasion like Easter or Christmas. Extra kudos for seasonal vegetables. If you have a cook to hand or are a bit cordon bleu yourself, then there is no excuse for your vegetables not to be 'barrelled' (the chefs' term being 'turned'), meaning they are formed in exactly the same barrel shape and size, thus ensuring even cooking while also being pleasing to the eye. His Majesty's vegetables are duly barrelled. Batons are a fine alternative, but make sure your carrots are never in rounds unless you are eating in the school canteen. Peas – even freshly shelled ones, really – are not part of a traditional British roast meal, although they are creeping in.

Finally, why do you rarely see cabbage or sprouts as part of the roast lunches in the best British homes? It is because a chemical found in both will make the silver cutlery (solid or plate) turn black.

Of course, nothing is more British than a roast meal, except the Brits coming up with rules for how their favourite savoury meal should be eaten for some to vehemently adhere to and for the rest to ignore.

Pudding versus dessert

A sweet and sticky bone of contention between upper-class and aspirational Brits and the rest of the world is the insistence on calling the final course of a meal 'pudding' rather than the globally more commonplace 'dessert'.

My American students will often comment that, to them, a pudding is a type of dessert (cooked in a pudding basin). This may be true in Charleston but it's de trop in Chelsea. Although most Brits now will use the words interchangeably, they were once very different. Puddings were heavy, flour-based staples of working-class kitchens: tasty morsels such as gooey treacle sponge, tart or moreish spotted dick. Desserts were elaborate, sweet confections served at the end of grand dinners in great houses, such as marchpanes, syllabubs and flummeries. These required greater culinary skill and were presented by aristocratic hosts to denote their status and show off the work of their kitchen staff.

Sugar became cheaper in the nineteenth century, and with the change from service à la française to the sequential service à la russe, these desserts started to be seen on middle-class dining tables, too. Shock horror! To maintain some social distinction, the aristocracy added a fruit course at the end of dinner, and called this 'dessert' and anything sweet a 'pudding'. At state banquets in Britain during the reign of Queen Elizabeth II, there was both a pudding and a dessert course, although the menus (then written in French) would herald 'fruits de dessert' to add some distinction between that and the less healthy course that preceded it. Away from the royal table, it still remains as a class differentiator: those who say pudding are seen as socially superior to those who say dessert.

Thirteen at dinner

As mentioned earlier, Brits have a charming aversion towards having thirteen at the dining table. The idea is that the first to leave the table when thirteen are gathered will be the first to die. This belief has surfaced repeatedly in Western popular culture, not just in the Bible, but with a prophecy by Professor Trelawney in *Harry Potter* and the Agatha Christie film *Thirteen at Dinner*.

For dinner and lunch parties, it's easy enough to make sure an even number is gathered, but for family events, short of asking younger members to hurriedly reproduce or adopt, it becomes tricky. This is where the teddy bear comes in (or it may be a wooden cat, in the instance of The Savoy, or – more sinisterly – a portrait). The table is set for fourteen, but a teddy bear is plonked on a chair, often with cushions to raise their eye line as they may as well see everyone. No one really questions this or passes much comment. It's just accepted as a perfectly normal custom of the British. And when no one dies directly following the meal, it's a win.

Conversation

In Regency England, where the seating plan would have been man-woman-man-woman exactly, a system was developed called 'turning the table'. This was when the hostess would speak with the gentleman on her left for the first course, then switch to the man on her right for the second, and then back to the left for course three, and so on. All other ladies followed suit. Maybe a camp little cough would be given between the courses to signal when it was time to turn. This conversational tennis ensured that everyone was spoken to fairly equally, especially if a handsome buck was seated next to a pretty, young ingénue on one side and an old trout on the other.

While it is rare to find exact man-woman-man-woman seating today, diners should remember this practice and try to share the love between the people sitting on either side of them. Speaking across the table used to be verboten, but mainly out of necessity as tables were much wider than they are today – they may even have had so many verdant floral arrangements down the middle of the table, they became a hedge, which somewhat limited both vision and conversation. Today, tables are narrower and often round, which lend themselves to sociability and can lead to group chat rather than a more regimented approach.

Dietary requirements

Who doesn't have a dietary requirement today? Are you even anyone if you aren't allergic or intolerant to something? You can't go five minutes in a restaurant without multiple staff asking if you have any allergies. My friend Jordan will always reply, 'Yes, to cats,' which causes momentary confusion for the waiters but seems to amuse him. Although it is preferable to the answer given by one stalwart British actor who, at the start of our lunch, replied grandly, 'Only to that question.' In the old days, of course, it was much easier as people just used to die. But while it is easy to scoff, I guess it's only good manners to try not to poison people.

The etiquette around dietary requirements (never just 'dietaries', please) has changed in recent years. Up until a decade ago, if you had anything for hosts to consider when menu planning, it was your responsibility to let them know when you accepted the invitation. Today, while the guest still needs to flag any requirements, good hosts should ask. And keep asking. I once had a surprise vegan for dinner, who four months previously had enjoyed beef Wellington at my table but now was a confirmed lover of the lentil but not of my lamb shank.

There is, of course, a difference between a dietary requirement and a food preference. I don't really like fish – in fact, I can't stand it – but if I were served it at someone's dinner I would do my very best to swallow as much as I could and think of England.

If you really don't like what is on your plate, eat as much as you can, push it to one side and make no comment or fuss.

Table service

Our upstairs-downstairs abilities are well known as a nation. Still to this day, British butlers command some of the best salaries in international private service, triumphing over equally skilled candidates from elsewhere purely because of their passport and accent. And as with everything, there is a British way of doing things when it comes to serving. Whether you are Carson, or fancy yourself as one, the principles are the same.

The international standard – borrowed (shock) from the US – is to serve food from the left-hand side of the diner and clear from the diner's right. But if you want to anglicise your buttling, know that it is the left-hand side from which we set and clear food – a standard pleasingly maintained in royal residences to this day. In private houses, plates are never balanced on the arm when brought from the kitchen, nor stacked on top of each other when clearing.

The right-hand side of the diner is only for the service of drinks – and, to be fair, this is the same in any country. As glassware is placed to the right-hand side of the setting, this makes sense. Make sure the lip of the bottle or carafe does not touch the rim of the glass when pouring. There's no need to lift the diner's glass off the table, either.

As with passing food, in Britain the table is served in a clockwise direction, starting with the guest of honour to the right of the host, then serving the host, and then the other guests to their left.

Never show up empty-handed: The duties of a guest

It could be argued that to be a good guest, you need to be a good host, as when being entertained, you will have empathy for the considerable workload and burden you and your fellow invitees are causing. Enjoying the hospitality of your host is all very well, but you must know it is good form to reciprocate unless you want the friendship to fizzle out. Reciprocity is a key trait in British diplomacy, both domestic and international. We will come to hosting shortly.

A big change in British etiquette in the last decade has been the dropping of the 'ten minutes late' rule, which was once so dutifully observed by older generations. Much of my childhood was spent sitting in one of my pathologically punctual parents' cars, clock-watching, waiting so we could arrive exactly ten minutes after the appointed hour. Their generations and the ones before created this rule to allow hosts to have a small buffer time where they could take a breath and do all those small jobs they may have missed before the onslaught of guests arrived. Now, more anxious millennials don't see any reason to observe this rule, worrying that if guests don't arrive on the dot of half seven that means they aren't coming at all and have stood their hosts up. That, or their time is so precious that arriving ten minutes late is a discourtesy. My suggestion for a happy compromise is – hardly revolutionarily, I grant you – arrive only five minutes late. Never, however, be early. As a host, I'd rather a guest was thirty minutes later than ten minutes early.

There are many cultures, however, that have a 'polychronic' approach to timekeeping (that's academic speak for 'late'). In Italy, for example, a dinner invitation may be for eight o'clock, but you can be sure you won't be eating until at least nine o'clock, if you're lucky, and probably half past nine.

But there will be occasions when guests are genuinely late. And we should say here that there is no such thing as 'fashionably late' – just plain damn rude. Indeed, with all the tech and information at our disposal today, there should never be any reason for anyone to be late again, especially in the absence of a message to the host to flag the tardiness, deliberate or otherwise. If a guest is running late, a modern touch would be to share their location from their phone so the host can see the accurate whereabouts of their guest and adjust any crucial timings accordingly. (And it saves the guest from having to worry about constantly updating their host on an ETA.)

I still have flashbacks to when I hosted some friends one Sunday evening, only for one single male friend not to arrive. After over an hour of waiting with no successful contact made, we agreed our hunger outweighed our concern, so went through and began enjoying my Carcassonne cassoulet. Thirty minutes later, the late friend strolled in, with no atonement for his whereabouts. I offered him the portion of the French stew that was left over, which he devoured, and then – when I brought out the pudding – he exclaimed, 'Oh, what, just the two courses?' He was not invited back and remains single to this day.

That fateful evening was host to a kitchen supper, which is a pared-down version of a dinner where heartier food is served and it doesn't go on as long. For these events, guests do not need to bring anything. But upon arrival at most other events, it is incorrect for a guest to show up empty-handed; a host gift must be proffered. Other exceptions to this rule would be any form of royal entertaining, drinks parties or corporate bashes.

Unless you know your hosts' exact taste in wine, turning up with a bottle or two is best avoided. It previously was thought to be a slight snub as you were implying that their wine selection was not good enough, although younger people with yet-to-mature tastes in wine are less fussed about this and are grateful for anything. But only bring wine if you know they will like it – don't just grab something from your own shelf as you put on your coat.

One host was slightly alarmed to be given a rare bottle of wine from a niche region of France that he knew his guests had never been to . . . yet he had visited last year and indeed presented his guests, when they had hosted several months earlier, with exactly the same bottle. Yet another good reason to think outside the case and bring something other than wine.

Champagne is more acceptable and is seen as less of a snub – but, as with wine, make sure you know they like it before you arrive holding your magnum. I abstained from all drink until I was twenty-three, but so many of my university friends would arrive for a candlelight supper at my flat eagerly clutching a bottle of wine for me, hoping I'd soon down their Pinot. Well-intended, but a non-gift. Chocolates are a more universal present – indeed, when this habit of host gifts arrived on British shores from America in the 1950s, chocolates were really the only correct thing to give. Flowers are an option, although only if they are already in an aqua bouquet. Cut flowers with exposed stems will mean that the poor host needs to put them in water immediately, and the floral-laden guest has just given their already overworked host a job within the first seven seconds of their arrival. Unless you go down the aqua bouquet route, send the flowers the day before, with a note attached saying how much you are looking forward to dinner. Your host can then take longer to display them, and many will be grateful for your contribution to the décor for the event.

Guests can think outside the box of chocolates and bring weird and wacky gifts, so long as they are tailored to the hosts. One considerate friend was once so concerned that I was skipping breakfast when I had to do long train journeys for work, she bought me a small click-and-lock plastic pot with a foldable 'spork' so I could take some fruit and yoghurt on my travels. To this day, however lavish or generous the other host gifts I have received, that remains the best. (On her next visit she bought me a pan scraper, however.)

Over in Japan, they like to bring fine cuts of steak to each other's houses as a gift. Thankfully, the habit of turning up with a prime chunk of top rump, however delicious it may prove to be, has not yet penetrated British shores.

Hosts should react favourably to any gift that is presented to them, even if they hate it or it's a total nuisance. There is always something to say without compromising ethics. 'Oh, what lovely packaging' is a personal favourite. Remember that any gift handed over to a host should not be expected to be seen again that evening by guests. The gift is for the hosts to enjoy at a later date and not opened and consumed that evening. Finally on gifts, hosts do not need to write to their guests to thank them for their host gifts.

Television programmes have led to a culture of guests thinking it is acceptable to have a quick fumble in the host's drawers and a poke around in their inglenook, but good manners say otherwise. Anything on display is fair game, however, so photographs on the mantle and assorted objets d'art are fine – but look, don't touch.

Unless a guest is planning on staying for the weekend, there is really no need for them to ask for the Wi-Fi password. You do not need the internet to make polite conversation with the real-life people around you. Hosts should make sure they make their Wi-Fi password as long, complicated and laborious as possible – not just for better encryption, but so guests who have been so rude as to ask for it get flustered and bored and give up on their attempt to stay connected to the digital world.

Don't run out of food: The duties of a host

Just as we judge strangers within seven seconds, the same principle applies to parties.

Guests who are greeted by red-faced hosts with glassy eyes and greasy aprons can probably be sure that they are not in for the most relaxed and convivial of evenings. Hosts should welcome guests to the bosoms of their banquets with nothing but relaxed merriment and gracious effervescence – even if they know it's all going to pot in the kitchen.

The good news is that anxious tension and enthusiasm both carry the same upbeat pace, so the former can be successfully masked as the latter if done deftly, but ideally a host has done so much preparation they can focus on warmly welcoming their guests, who have begun to arrive on time.

While you may be forgiven for silently plotting different types of pain you could inflict on any guests who do arrive early, you can't show any rage. A friend told me a story where she arrived at a dinner at the requested time of seven o'clock, only to have the host scream 'I actually meant half seven' in her face and slam the door shut. Needless to say, the host had not graduated from any finishing school.

Once guests are inside, hopefully calmly, a host should offer to assist them out of any coats. At a terribly polite British dinner party a friend once went to, the guests were assembled in the sitting room still wearing their coats for ten minutes before the host realised their mistake. They had all been too polite and didn't like to mention it or cause a fuss.

The art of easing someone out of their coat is a skill that requires attention to detail:

- Hold the coat at the midpoint of each shoulder, making sure you do not let the hemline touch the floor. (This can be impossible for very long coats, however.)
- Close the coat so the lining isn't showing and fold it over your arm.
- Hang on a decent-width coat hanger, not a thin, wiry one from the dry cleaner's, if possible.

We'd all like to think we have proper cloakrooms and hanging space to take care of each guest's outerwear, but many people don't. Lying a blanket across a nearby bed and carefully arranging the coats is a decent alternative in the circumstances.

Assisting someone out of their coat is one thing; making them undress any further is an imposition. It is not correct to ask dinner guests to remove their shoes, and nor is it really good manners for guests to do it without prompting. This is one of the great social dividers in Britain. A shoe is part of the entire ensemble and remains on the respective foot. Can you imagine people arriving for a reception at Buckingham Palace and being asked to shed their shoes, with Queen Camilla handing out white fluffy slippers?

There are, as ever, exceptions to the rule. If your shoe is caked in fresh, wet mud, or they have just traipsed across a blanket of fallen red berries from a nearby tree, it is probably best to flag and await a host's decision as to whether they want the shoes carefully removed. Hosts should indicate to their guests if they have a particular preference – no guest wants to be the only shoe-on or shoe-off person at the party.

If a host is entertaining in a mosque or a temple, then it's fair enough to get everyone to go barefooted. In all other instances, in traditional British manners, it still remains a bit vulgar and down-market to have a shoes-off policy. If you are that concerned about the welfare of your Grade One Axminster, don't have guests over. Hosts who do insist on no shoes indoors should make sure there is a nearby bench or handy pouffe for guests to sit on. As a guest, if there is no seat, if you do get instructed to remove your shoes, then naturally oblige, but make a huge performance of losing your balance, and having to lean on walls and other guests in order for your host's maddening request to be fulfilled.

Perhaps this British snobbery over shoes has its origins, like most things, in class? Upper- and upper-middle-class houses usually have wooden or stone floors, covered with rugs. Their sort also tend to have a much less materialistic approach to possessions and décor in general. Whereas the middle class and below love a wall-to-wall carpet and therefore can get prissy.

Once de-coated (and maybe de-shoed too), guests should be brought into the main thrum of the party and introduced, if they do not know any or many of the assembled throng. As stated earlier, some context should be given by the host about each individual involved in the introduction, to lubricate the start of the conversation.

If you look up 'gauche' in the dictionary, you will find this given as a definition: offering guests a tour of your house, as if it were in the National Trust collection. The only possible exception is if you have just moved into a new house and it has some particularly notable features and architectural quirks. A new 55-inch curved OLED television in the 'living room' does not qualify. Guests on the receiving end of such an offer should reply, 'Oh, it's all right, no rush, I wouldn't want to distract you from the cooking,' but then give in if the matter is pushed, in order to be polite. Try to muster up as much enthusiasm as possible as you are shown the new home for the Billy bookcase, and the inevitable accent wall behind the bed.

Hosts trying to climb the British social ladder should make sure suitable pictures are on display. Should you own a snap of you meeting any key public figures (royal, diplomatic or government; celebrities don't count), then make sure they are not front and centre but rather tucked away, as if it is no great consequence that you met the Duke of Sussex. Which it really wouldn't be, anyway.

There is an increased laxity with departure times today, but while it is poor form for guests to outstay their welcome, hosts should take it as a great compliment that their guests do not want to leave. Although I do wonder if socially anxious millennial guests just don't want to be the first to upset the apple cart and leave – usually highlighted when one plucks up the courage and then everyone suddenly has the same idea, thankful they were not the first, creating a mass exodus that brings the party to a very sudden close rather than a more elegant decrescendo. Sometimes a host does need to drop a few hints to subtly usher people to the door. Although when the hosts start doing the dishes, clearly all the more nuanced hints have been missed.

My social circle has heard me talk about this topic one too many times in the media, and they now know that when I announce, 'Can I get anyone anything else?' it is a thinly veiled plea for them to get the hint and begin making tracks. While my friends may know what that means, I do encourage people to use that on their own guests as I am sure they may not pick up on the passive-aggression as quickly. Another good one is 'Have you got a very busy day tomorrow?' Getting their minds onto what they have planned is better for a quick departure than if you keep serving drinks and food.

To assist someone back into their coat:

- Check the sleeves, in case of a scarf or gloves.
- Make sure the coat is positioned so the person can easily slip their arms into the sleeves (as with taking the coat off, try to avoid it trailing on the floor).
- Lift the coat on, and then lift it again to settle it comfortably over the clothes underneath.
- Make sure the collar of the garment underneath is hidden by the collar of the coat.

The host book

Popular also in France and the US, a host book is a record of what was served and to whom. For anyone who wishes to become the host with the most, acquiring one of these hardbacked volumes is a must. Not only do they ensure you don't offer meatballs twice in a row to a return guest, but they also serve as wonderful sources of party nostalgia later in life – and they make for an original wedding gift if you know the couple like entertaining.

Each double-page spread has the same layout. On one side, a blank space for the table to be drawn out, with each guest's initials marking where they sat. On the other side, usually in two columns, is where the names are written out in full, plus the menu, including drinks served and – for the florally minded – a note on what flowers.

Next time a guest returns, they will get a fresh menu, sit next to different people if there's any overlap, and not have to endure staring at very similar drab carnations.

Houseguests

We're probably all aware of the bon mot from Benjamin Franklin: 'Guests, like fish, begin to smell after three days.' A similar rule of thumb is that you should never stay with people who you wouldn't want to stay in your own house. Sadly, the exception to this rule is family.

Upon accepting the invitation to stay, guests must alert their hosts to any allergies or intolerances they may have – this can range from being gluten-free to being deathly allergic to feathers. If you do have a known bedding-related medical condition, it may be a good thing to suggest you bring your own pillows or bedding, should your hosts not have any synthetic-fibre equivalents. If hosts have the space and budget, keeping some hypoallergenic or fully allergy-proof bedding for sensitive guests is always a good idea. Washing guest bedding with non-biological washing detergent is also good practice, as biological detergents can make people's skin break out in rashes.

If your host asks you what time you'd like breakfast in the morning, the correct answer is 'What time would suit?' or 'Whatever time you normally eat'. The question is rhetorical and not actually meant to give you a choice. Remember you are not at an hotel but a private house. Once a time has been agreed, make sure you show up a few moments before, if not sooner, so you can offer to help in the final stages. Unless you are part of a hen party, shower and change out of your pyjamas before breakfast is served if you want to be invited back.

No one should ever be too grand to offer help to their hosts, and hopefully no host will ever be so grand they continually refuse it. Ask to help set the table, or help wash or dry up after dinner. If you are staying for more than four days (your poor hosts), you should not expect your hosts to foot the bill for all meals. Instead, offer to cook (and buy the ingredients) – or, better still, invite them out to a local restaurant as your guests; then they won't need to tidy up after you.

Upon their departure, thoughtful guests will ask whether they should strip the bed before leaving, regardless of who the host is or how many staff the house has. Good hosts would never dream of asking guests to do this, but should appreciate the offer of help. If you have been staying in a house with staff, especially staff that have been looking after you and your room, then in many houses it is the done thing to leave a tip for them when you leave. Ask your hosts whether this is all right, and if so, what amount they suggest.

Now, please pay attention, hosts; let us make the most important matter clear. A clean guestroom is not a luxury, it is a must. Your guests should expect to be sleeping in clean comfort. Dirt may not faze you, but for anyone with an iota of sanitariness, it will freak them out, even if they say nothing.

Although ultimately down to personal preference, white bedding works best for guest beds as it can go with any colour scheme, looks inviting (so long as it is clean), and will last however many times you decide to redecorate. Many find it the most soothing and relaxing – and that is a key purpose of a bedroom.

But whatever the colour or pattern, make sure it's ironed. You can't provide good hospitality with creased sheets. Even if you don't iron your own bedding, do please iron the guests'. I had a strictly adhered-to standard never to get in between any bedding that wasn't ironed, which is perhaps why I was single for many years. But I was glad to keep the British end up.

The author Mary Killen once advised hosts not to bother changing the bedsheets themselves between guests but, instead, to leave a pile of clean bedding on a chair in the guest room. In Mary's world, the host could then apologise for not getting around to it and suggest the guest do it themselves, in the hope that they don't care and just climb in. Disgusting. This is not correct etiquette. If you don't want to play B&B, don't invite anyone.

While plenty of surface, wardrobe and drawer space in the guest room is a must, a simple and hospitable touch is a carafe of water and some glasses – or, failing the carafe, some bottles (although bottles of mineral water can make it look more like an hotel than a private residence). Fill the carafe just before the guest is due to arrive, or else the vessel will have water bubbles, which show just how long it has been sitting there. Yuck.

A decent mirror, two bedside tables and at least two free and convenient plug sockets are also musts for guest bedrooms, where space allows.

As with bedding, white is often a smart colour of choice for bathroom towels, as it makes the towels look so much more inviting than dingy beige or depressing stone grey. Two towels per person is the correct number to offer – a smaller 'head' towel plus a larger one for the body. As noted by renowned hotelier Alex Polizzi, there is a trend in hotels, which has infiltrated houses, to put the towels piled up on the bed when there is a perfectly good towel rail in the bathroom. Such hotels and hosts may as well put the duvet in the bath.

Before hosts welcome any guests, especially after a house move or a major refurbishment, it is wise to spend a night or two sleeping in the guest room to iron out any teething issues – is there a plug near the mirror for a hair dryer, for example? Critically, is there a bin available for both dry and wet items? When I had 'etiquette Granny' to stay with me one year, she marched me out of the flat the next morning to the nearest department store to find me a wastepaper basket for the bedroom for 'dry items'. Clearly, without one, she had had a trying and restless night having to endure sleeping in the hellhole that was my guest suite.

A nice bit of crumpet: Tea

If fish and chips or roast beef are meant to be the best of British food, surely a scone and a cup of tea must be giving their savoury competition a run for their money? While every hotel tea menu will give a few lines of history thanking Anna Maria Russell, wife to the seventh Duke of Bedford, for inventing tea, the reality is that Anna didn't do an awful lot when it comes to the now worldwide phenomenon that is 'afternoon tea'. Whisper it quietly, but a French aristocrat is said to have introduced afternoon tea to her Paris salon in 1837, four years before said Duchess of Bedford. And evidence of the habit of tea-drinking accompanied by some munchettes goes back as far as 1758.

But while there are three silver tiers' worth of evidence that Anna Maria did not 'invent' afternoon tea, she certainly played an important role in making a habit of taking tea in the afternoon – then at around five o'clock. Though Anna Maria and her female associates would only have enjoyed a refreshing cup of tea with some lightly buttered bread. Do not for one minute think they were all tucking into delicate patisserie and scones.

The buttered bread would either have been like the finger sandwiches we know today, but without the filling, or one slice of bread, buttered and rolled in on itself. Both were designed to prevent ladies from developing clumsiness, aka 'butter fingers'. Their bread was crustless not for daintiness but because the loaves then available were of the cob or cottage variety (think a large crusty bread roll). This meant the crusts had to be cut off to make those neat fingers or rolls, and so the crustless sandwich we associate with a modern afternoon tea was born.

Hotels and tea houses began to get in on the act around 1865, offering this patrician repast to the growing middle classes. The Langham in London was, reportedly, the first hotel to offer afternoon tea, although – again – it was miles off the cardiac event waiting to happen that many endure today. It wasn't until The Ritz revived it in the 1980s that what we now recognise as afternoon tea began to take shape, with other hotels realising they had a big gap between lunch and dinner and 'afternoon tea' would put some derrières on Davenports and give the hotel's expensive pastry chefs something to do. But all this history is less than clear-cut and a bit waffly, so as antiques doyen and historian Steven Moore often says, 'It is no wonder people prefer to ignore the facts and believe it was all down to a hungry duchess.'

While the history of afternoon tea in hotels is more recent than many think, families in grand private houses did enjoy a late afternoon snack around the turn of the twentieth century. Everyone would congregate in a drawing room for tea at five o'clock, the butler and footman having laid a table at one side with the required paraphernalia. Children would be brought down by their governess or nanny to see their parents, and any guests staying with the family would also join. Having all the 'upstairs' in one room for an hour enabled the 'downstairs' to have free run of the house, getting the bedrooms and dressing rooms ready for dinner, tidying whatever needed to be tidied, and not getting in anyone's way – or, more to the point, not having anyone get in their way. The staff of a house would then have their tea, sometimes called 'high tea' as it was served on a high table, around six o'clock, before the big dinner-service push. It was a more substantial meal than what the upstairs had.

Sandwiches would have been square, however, rather than rectangular – and still are, in private service. We aren't sure why or when this preference of shape came about, although there is a strong rumour that a former king didn't like the rectangular shape as it reminded him of coffins, so ordered his kitchens to forever more present square sandwiches.

In the Royal Household, tea is still served for all levels of the family and household, although again, it is a pared-down version of what royal subjects and tourists eat in the surrounding hotels of London.

Problem guests

While we may all love each of our friends individually for who they are and want to tolerate their quirks and unique personality traits, sometimes they can let us down with their comportment during our generous hospitality. Whether it's not knowing their own limits with alcohol and getting so squiffy it stops being faintly amusing and starts being annoying, or they think it's okay to be inappropriate with others, our guest list can disgrace themselves and leave a blot on our party landscape. Of course, every transgression is different, and the context and motivations for each will require a distinct and different approach. It is hard to give all-encompassing advice on how to handle every situation, but common sense and compassion are the watchwords.

While putting the bottle of wine on the table is a relaxed cue for guests to help themselves, it usually leads to people getting trolleyed quicker than if the host regulates the pouring throughout the meal. (Guests, if you note the bottles are on the side, don't go and help yourself.) Regardless of where the bottle has been living, guests who are quicker on their way to inebriation should stop being served immediately, unless it's to provide them with reservoirs of water or coffee.

As Brits never like to make a scene, it's best to remove the miscreant from the room as quickly and quietly as possible. Should you need to make them feel the rough edge of your tongue, this must never be done in front of the other guests. While the culprit may be in the wrong, it is equally as wrong to admonish them publicly, making them lose face.

For single guests who get too merry and start causing an unpleasant scene, it's best to put them in a taxi and send them home, unless you have a spare bed. Taxi apps are very helpful today for this, as you can make sure you put in their home address, track their journey, and know that they won't need to drunkenly faff with cash or cards at the other end. Don't worry too much about what you say to them, as it is highly likely they won't remember it anyway.

Guests who decide that illegal drugs in someone else's house are their way to enjoy the evening should have a host's utmost pity before the host's utmost fury. Bringing such substances into anyone's private space is the greatest social solecism, and there is very little a guest can do to backtrack from such an act of idiocy. Aside from being illegal, which should be reason enough for anyone in sound mind not to do something, middle-class drug-takers always fall back on the defence that it is 'recreational' – a word that does a lot of heavy lifting and that their addled minds have decided somehow makes it all okay. (Next, we'll all be told, 'Don't worry, I'm only a *recreational* murderer.') It is totally lost on them that to fuel their 'recreational' habit, someone further down the supply chain is living a life of poverty, being trafficked, abused and god-knows-what-else. Meanwhile, middle-class consumers enjoy a cosy lifestyle, their disposable income fuelling crime and causing horrific deforestation in the drug's country of origin.

But, let us go back to pity and compassion. On the provision and promise that the spectacular lapse in judgement from the guest is never repeated, we once again look to Dame Maggie Smith's indomitable Lady Grantham in *Downton Abbey* for our approach: 'Forgive, perhaps; forget, never.'

General procedure for wedding guests

The etiquette of modern weddings would be enough to fill a separate book – and maybe one day will – but some advice is needed on what is correct and what is not correct for guests at the weddings we have all come to know and love/hate today.

As Graham Norton says, 'Modern weddings are designed to annoy people.' How so? Perhaps because family life for the couple getting married is more complicated than it was fifty-plus years ago, which leads to highly contentious seating plans and other politics. (I once attended a wedding where the receiving line was comically long, due to there being so many parents and step-parents. The couple had clearly, and rather sweetly, wanted to include everyone and not let anyone feel left out, but at the expense of common sense and ease.) Or maybe weddings annoy others because many of our British traditions are being lost as we import ones (some good, some horrid) from other countries? Or because social media and the rise in everyone craving their moment in the matrimonial spotlight has such a stranglehold on so many of us?

Before I walk you down the aisle of matrimonial manners, I should disclose that I am not the biggest fan of weddings, but I shall try to be as impartial and compassionate as possible when discussing the courtesies guests should keep in mind. The advice that follows is not tied to any particular religion, denomination or lack thereof, but applies generally to weddings of any creed, shape or size.

While we will discuss dress codes at length later, guests should know that it is not good form to decide to wear something different than what is asked of you on the invitation. That said, correctly, traditional British wedding invitations don't actually ever state a dress code. Though when that rule was codified (not recently, I hasten to add), the idea was that weddings were morning dress occasions, and that was that. Today, not everyone has morning dress – or knows what it is.

For my own wedding, where the invitations followed a traditional format, no dress code was printed but we did give sartorial direction on the additional information slip that was included when the invitations (never 'invites') were sent. Most people like to know what to wear, and telling them explicitly always helps to avoid having people rock up dressed totally inappropriately, which will not relax them and, frankly, can ruin photographs. If guests have not been told what the dress code is, however, it is perfectly acceptable for them to ask the couple or any of the key players. Better to get it right than guess.

While many wedding guests dress more informally today, the old rules for guests not wearing black or white still apply. Some say the modern exception to this would be a same-sex wedding of two men where there is no bride. In theory, wearing white would be okay unless the couple are having bridesmaids or the equivalent, who may be wearing some form of white or cream fabric. Black is funereal and always will be, so don't think you can get away with it, please. The only exception would be if the wedding dress code is black tie, but that only applies to the dinner jackets for men, so LBDs are still de trop. (And black-tie weddings are distinctly transatlantic.)

When guests arrive at the ceremony venue, one hopes there will be ushers to guide people to where they should sit. Convention-ally, the bride's family and friends sit on the left of the venue (as you walk up the aisle), and the groom's on the right. With same-sex couples, or where friends do not 'belong' to one side or the other, usually anything goes. Regardless of whether there are set sides, the front few rows should always be reserved for family, and ushers should be briefed accordingly, especially if there are no reserved signs.

Forget wedding bells or pews bedecked with peonies, nothing pro-vides a greater sense of occasion at a wedding than the officiant telling guests not to post on social media until the couple has. If no such instruction is given, however, good guests should still be care-ful about what they post and when. A good rule of thumb would be that posting photos of yourself and friends is fine, but posting anything featuring the couple or key aspects of their special day is best avoided until they themselves have posted or given you per-mission. Always best to check first, if in doubt. As potentially narcissistic as it is, with modern weddings being as ridiculously expensive as they are, you can understand why couples might want to have first dibs on revealing key aspects of their day to other people online. However, it always amuses me that the couples who strictly insist on this are forgetting that they're being dictatorial about showing themselves off to people they didn't like or care about enough to invite in the first place.

It is not good manners, however, to get guests to surrender their mobile phones for the duration of the wedding in the interests of privacy, however grand or famous the couple is – or think they are. If you can't trust your guests not to leak anything or post things before you or whatever magazine you've done a deal with, don't invite them.

Guests should have some loose change to hand for any retiring collection there may be at the end of the ceremony, especially if it is in a church, where a silver dish may be passed around. As one acerbic vicar said, 'We do prefer notes as coins do so scratch the plate.'

When moving from ceremony to reception, there is now often a guestbook to sign. This is a more recent innovation in terms of weddings, and older generations may not know there even is one. Any master of ceremonies or a person speaking during the wedding breakfast is best to direct guests who are yet to wield a nib to do so. Unlike with visitor books in historic houses, where you are only meant to sign your name and nothing else, wedding guests are meant to write a gushing sentence of adoration and love in the wedding book.

Another new 'tradition' for British weddings is wedding cards, which are the contemporary version of the telegrams that were sent ahead by guests unable to attend to be read out on the day by the father of the bride. Today, guests don't have to bring a card if they don't want to; they can opt to send one in the post instead. Whenever you issue your card, pen something congratulatory and thank the couple (again) for the invitation, and try to include a personal story or joke.

Remember that a wedding card is not a substitute for a thank-you letter after the day itself. If money is being given as a gift, arrange this separately via 'official' channels set up by the couple rather than leave an envelope of cash lying around the reception venue.

One good test of how British you really are is whether you got a bit squeamish just then when I mentioned giving money as a gift. Traditional Brits will not like this, as any public or private display of finance is always tricky. Money is such a divisive issue and one we try to avoid at all costs. But even in the UK attitudes are – very slowly – beginning to change on giving money to a couple getting married.

Traditionally, a gift registry was because the couple had not cohabited and, after their wedding day, would be setting up their first home together, so needed a dinner service, fondue set and a pie slice. Today, couples have often lived together for years and may have had one or two homes already, so there's no need for additional pie slices. In such instances, asking for actual gifts can seem greedy, which is probably why the more modern trend of asking for cash has developed. Although many see it as a more recent innovation, close family would have traditionally given some money to the couple getting married. For most weddings now, this has been extended to any wedding guest having to give a bit of cash. For couples who don't want a gift registry and don't feel comfortable asking for money, it is a smart idea to suggest guests donate to a chosen charity instead.

Whether it's money or the fondue set, there is no obligation for guests to buy or give anything to the couple, especially if the guest has had to pay for travel and accommodation as well as take time off work to attend the wedding. The exception to this would be if the guest is a millionaire, where a parsimonious attitude would look stingy. Wedding gifts should not be brought to the wedding itself, however, but sent before or after the day, if the services of a gift-list company are not being used.

As the wedding draws to a close – and most weddings today drag on for at least two hours too long – guests should avoid making a 'French exit' unless they really have to. (I was once so unwell at a wedding that the sight of the 'doughnut wall' made me quite bilious, and I had to leave immediately.) Guests should make sure they have thanked and said goodbye to the couple – and, if easily accessible, the respective parents of the couple, too.

Once home, a thank-you letter should be sent. Specific advice on these can be found on page 169, but traditionally you only wrote to the parents of the bride, as they were the ones hosting, as written on the invitations. Today, weddings are, in effect, crowd-funded, so several thank-you letters should be written – one to the newlyweds, and one to each set of parents, if you know they had some involvement in the planning and/or funding.

CHAPTER SIX

She Was a Barker, He Was a Finch; Suddenly They're Hyphenated

'Call me Jim,' said the newly installed Secretary for Administrative Affairs.

'I would prefer to call you Minister, Minister,' his advisor chirruped. A quick exchange from the BBC sitcom *Yes, Minister*, but one that, in a nutshell, summarises the British obsession with titles and rank. That programme was set and made in the 1980s, and British life, especially political life, has dramatically changed. If you compare *Yes, Minister* to its twenty-first-century counterpart, *The Thick of It*, how the civil service and special advisors addressed their ministers would make Sir Humphrey and Bernard Woolley pack up and head for Pyongyang in desperate search of much-missed deference.

While the characters in *The Thick of It* may be extreme in their laxity in observing correct form, how normal (real) Brits are with it today is somewhere in the middle of the two political satires. We get it, we know we need it, we use it, but we don't use it all the time. There is almost now a requisite disrespect for nomenclature in modern Britain.

Away from the establishment, the 1960s and 1970s saw deference firmly abandoned in favour of a freer and more casual approach to people and their given or assumed status. After the election of New Labour in 1997, everyone was told to call the prime minister by his first name instead of his rank. He was to be addressed as we do our friends and pets, rather than the person who was in charge of keeping us on the straight and narrow. This rise in informality has led to a rise in inaccuracies and blissful ignorance.

Britain is a funny old country, as is probably very clear now to everyone reading this book. We are the only country that has television news programmes incorrectly label someone of a supposed elevated rank, and also have people notice and fly into a fit of pique at the stupidity. Take the great composer Andrew Lloyd Webber, who in 1997 was made a life peer and given the title of baron, thus becoming Lord Lloyd-Webber.* Whenever he appears on television, his name strap will invariably read 'Lord Andrew Lloyd-Webber'. If you are new to the world of British correct form, especially for the peerage, you may not see what is wrong with that. If you are an old pro, however, you may have thrown this book across the room.

Styling any peer using his title, first name and surname is wrong. That styling is reserved for the younger sons of dukes and marquesses. What would be correct for the television captions to write would be 'Lord Lloyd-Webber'. Brits expect our broadcast industry to get these things correct, and Andrew should be accorded the correct rank. Or else what was the point in him being given it?

* The composer of *Phantom of the Opera* now has a hyphen in his surname (Lloyd-Webber) as the House of Lords insists on hyphens for double-barrelled names, even though on his birth certificate he is Lloyd Webber, with no hyphen. Only such a small detail would matter in Britain!

British broadcasting services also have rules as to who gets a name strap and who doesn't. While change may be coming, generally on the BBC in the UK, only the King, members of the Royal Family, the prime minister, the pope and the president of the United States appear without a strap-on, whereas everyone else who appears on the news has one.

Away from forms of address, how we communicate more generally has changed. Most see letter-writing as something terribly laborious and a total effort, which is why only scant advice will be given here on how to put pen to paper. For all business communications and a large majority of social ones, the online world is preferred.

For those who like to run their thumbs over engraved stiff ones, sadly it's no longer a given for the guests of weddings and grand parties to receive proper, formal invitations. How we as a country invite people to our birthdays and celebrations has changed, bringing with it some uncertainty and lack of clarity – due to, arguably, too much innovation.

Britain can still lead the way in all this, however. While we may be less hung up on how to address a bishop during Lent, and where we should stick Andrew Lloyd Webber's hyphen (or not), we now have inclusive language and ensuring we do not offend or misgender someone to worry about, just like we used to worry about demoting a baron to the younger son of an earl. New rules are needed for a new way of life, to reflect the more diverse range of people that walk amongst us, as well as our love for mannerly monikers.

Terms of address

As etiquette evolves, the rules of correct form have become less clear-cut than they once were. Society and attitudes have changed to include groups of people who were previously excluded or ignored. We now have a much richer, more diverse and interesting world because of it. Some people are still unsure how to address others, which is understandable. But ignorance is not an excuse for repeat offences.

There are now different honorifics to use, such as 'Ms' and 'Mx'. The former is still tricky in some instances. An equal number of women will be offended if you don't style them 'Ms' as there are women who would be livid if you do.

Conventionally, we say 'Mr and Mrs', of course. But I receive many questions from students and correspondents asking what is wrong with writing 'Mrs and Mr'. Other than citing 'convention', it's a tricky question to answer rationally without sounding slightly chauvinistic. My take? It's totally fine if you or someone you're writing to wants it that way. So be it. It doesn't worry me and it shouldn't worry anyone secure enough in their own skin and position.

The best catch-all advice for life today is if you are in any doubt as to how to style someone's name, ask them. A person can be a different style at different times, depending on the context. They may be styled differently at work than in their private lives. The style that is most appropriate for the circumstance should be chosen. For example, in the workplace, a woman may be 'Ms Susan Smith', but in her social life, she may style herself 'Mrs John Smith'.

Making a note in your address book or the contacts section in your phone as to which titles each person in your life prefers is a sensible way to help you remember to get it right each time you correspond with them. A little courtesy goes a long way. One divorced friend said she more or less 'held it together' immediately following her decree absolute, until I sent her a text to ask what honorific and styling she would prefer going forward for her birthday card. I hasten to add she was moved to tears not because I was hammering home the fact she was now divorced but because 'no one has shown me that level of consideration for quite some time'.

If someone addresses you incorrectly, correct them nicely. One of the basics of good manners around correct form is that your name belongs to you, and everyone is entitled to be addressed as they prefer.

I am often asked whether or not to dot (place a full stop, or period, after the honorific). British manners like finicky details like this. But the answer depends on where you are in the world. Some countries are dottier than others. In Britain, or what is now bizarrely termed 'UK English', we do not place dots or full stops after 'Mr', 'Mrs', 'Ms', 'Mstr' or the like. In 'US English', however, they do.

This book is not for those who need detailed advice on how to address people with aristocratic or diplomatic titles, however. There are many excellent resources available, some of which are listed in the bibliography. Having said all of the above about new forms of address and changing attitudes to nomenclature, the conventional guidelines are usually correct and a good place to start when it comes to how to address people.

Untitled people

Beginning with the conventional, let me take you on the journey of Peter and Jane and how they would be styled in writing and speech as they progress along the rollercoaster we call life. And, brace yourselves, because for these two in particular, there are a lot of highs and lows.

When Peter pops into the world, he is styled as 'Mstr Peter Smith' on envelopes and invitations and 'Master Smith' in formal speech, but realistically just 'Peter'.

Over in the next hospital bed, Jane's successfully made her way out of the birth canal and is now accorded the written style 'Miss Jane Jones' and 'Miss Jones' or 'Jane' in speech.

In the old days, Peter would stop being a master and become a mister when he came of age.* But you try calling a fifteen-year-old today 'Master' and see how they like it. This is a rule that has been adjusted, and now when a boy reaches the age of twelve, it's probably safer to drop 'Master'. And so, 'Mr Peter Smith' it is from this point on when he is written to, and 'Mr Smith' in conversation.

To make it easier for us, Peter is not the most academically gifted man, and so in the course of his life, does not gain any medical qualifications or academic accolades. His honorific remains 'Mister', bypassing any chance to be a 'Doctor' of either variety or 'Professor'. Sorry, Peter. He therefore remains 'Mr Peter Smith' for the rest of his life.

Jane, on the other hand, remains 'Miss Jane Jones' and 'Miss Jones' even once she comes of age. If she died without marrying, this is – conventionally – how she would be styled. But Peter and Jane have an accidental encounter one day, not knowing they both entered the world on the same day, just one bed apart. They bump into each other at the local petrol station, and their eyes meet while Peter pumps unleaded into his hatchback. Jane's legs go all

---

* In the UK, ages of majority are all over the place. A person can join the army at sixteen but can't drive a car until a year later, and still can't exercise their democratic right for a further twelve months. Officially, the legal age of majority is eighteen.

wobbly as she realises that she is bored of filling her own tank each month and maybe needs someone to take turns with. She makes the first move and strikes up a conversation with Peter as they queue at the checkout waiting to pay.

A coffee date soon follows, then a dinner, and a cosy night in at Jane's watching *The Shining* (her choice). They both decide at very similar times that they are destined to be together forever. Jane beats Peter to it and proposes.

Months go by as they plan their wedding, almost coming to blows with Jane's mother, who has very odd views on the font used for the orders of service; then, once the celebrant has done their thing, the couple are styled together on paper as 'Mr and Mrs Peter Smith', 'Mr and Mrs Smith' in conversation, and on her own, Jane becomes 'Mrs Peter Smith' in writing and 'Mrs Smith' in speech. She may have proposed and enjoy horror films, but Jane decides to take her husband's surname and has no problem with his first name being used in formal writing when they are addressed together. This is how they will be styled for the rest of their happily married life, including after their two point four lovely children are brought into the world.

After a wonderful honeymoon in South Africa, except for the mouse that finds its way into the bedroom, Jane returns to work. Not wanting to confuse everyone (her colleagues can be quite dense at times) and knowing her marital status has no bearing on her ability to fulfil the job description, she decides to keep being known as 'Jane Jones' in her professional life, but uses 'Ms' as her honorific going forward.

Life is going well for Peter and Jane.

But, plot twist: Peter and Jane fall out of love.

Peter is one day back at the same petrol station at which he met his now wife and sees a woman filling up an electric-blue sports car. He decides he fancies a younger model and starts an illicit affair with this other woman. A divorce is inevitable.

The patriarchy being what it is, Peter remains styled as he was when he came of age. He is still 'Mr Peter Smith' in writing and 'Mr Smith' in speech. His marital status – married or divorced – has not changed anything.

But it's a different story for Jane. The good news is, however, that – as well as custody of the children – she has options. For the sake of an easy life with childcare, Jane could choose to retain her ex-husband's last name, but she would not use his first name. Option one is that she is styled 'Mrs Jane Smith' on envelopes and invitations and is still 'Mrs Smith' in speech. Or, if she really can't even stand the thought of her cheating ex, she can be styled as 'Miss Jane Jones' and 'Miss Jones' – back to how she was before she married. (For either option, Jane could use 'Ms' instead of 'Miss' or 'Mrs', too, if she wanted.)

For all those Peter and Jane fans who wanted it to work out, let's just imagine a parallel universe where they buy a fully electric car once married, so Peter doesn't ever need to go to the petrol station and never sees the younger model. Peter and Jane remain married forever. Until Peter dies. (It was painless.)

Traditionally, Jane would remain on paper as 'Mrs Peter Smith' as, in the eyes of the law, she is still married to Peter. Even though he's now dead and sprinkled round the local common. That's English law for you. But some widows prefer not to have a reminder of their dead love, and so drop their husband's first name and are styled as (traditionally) a divorced woman would be: 'Mrs Jane Smith'.

Jane's friends are unsure how she wants to be styled as Jane hasn't brought it up or given it much thought, so they style all sympathy cards and letters 'Mrs Peter Smith' until Jane politely tells them otherwise.

The use of 'Ms'

As with our now close friend Jane above, working women often use the Ms honorific as their marital status has no bearing on their job. 'Miss' and 'Mrs' can also be used, but the woman's first name is stated. Thus, 'Miss/Mrs/Ms Jane Smith'.

'Ms' became popular in the 1980s after the *New York Times* started using it, although it dates to 1901, when it was first proposed as an honorific for women who didn't want to denote their marital status. While some say 'Ms' dates back even further, most scholars believe those earlier uses of 'Ms' are abbreviations for 'Miss' or 'Mrs' (both of which are short forms of 'Mistress*').

For those formally writing to working women, 'Ms' should always be used unless you are absolutely sure you know 'Miss' or 'Mrs' is acceptable. There should be no stigma around the use of 'Ms' in any context, whether social or business. Indeed, for the royal wedding of Prince Harry and Meghan Markle, on the invitations, which were issued from the then Prince of Wales, 'Ms' was used for the first time in public-facing royal correspondence, finally marking the end to any silly taboo around its use. As we note from the Royal Household, 'Ms' can now be used socially, too – often, but not always, by those who have gone through a divorce and feel that 'Miss' makes them appear too young.

* Until the nineteenth century, there was no connotation of whether a woman was married or not. 'Mistress', often abbreviated to 'Mrs', was used for women of a higher status or for older women, regardless of their marital status.

Same-sex couples

There are so few etiquette books (anywhere in the world) that address the styling of same-sex couples. Given that in the UK homosexuality was finally made legal in 1967, you'd have thought that in the nearly sixty years since, someone might have deemed it sensible to print some advice. Let us right that wrong.

As with heterosexual couples, some homosexual couples retain their individual surnames rather than choosing one over the other. In such an instance, the names are styled alphabetically by surname: 'Mr Julian Brown and Mr Sandy White'. The same convention applies to two women or two non-binary people – use the alphabet.

You can also use the rather old-fashioned but grand styling of 'Messrs' (pronounced to rhyme with 'lezzers' – I really can't think of any other word it rhymes with), which is the anglicised version of 'Messieurs'. Thus: 'Messrs Brown and White'. If one has taken the surname of the other, then you organise the first names by alphabetical order: 'Mr Julian and Mr Sandy Brown'.

For two women, the same logic above is followed, but 'Mr' and 'Mssrs' get substituted for either 'Miss', 'Ms' or 'Mrs' depending on marital status and their personal choice, and 'Mmes' or 'Mses', which are short for 'Mesdames' and 'Mademoiselles'.

For two married non-binary people, exactly the same conventions are followed (use the alphabet), but the honorifics are 'Mx' and 'Mxes'.

Students of the finer points of correct form have started to ponder whether the male spouses of knights of the realm and other members of the titled classes receive a courtesy title, as with heterosexual female spouses. The simple answer is a regretful 'no'. For example, there is no such thing as Lord David Furnish, or Lord David John . . . much to their probable disappointment. He remains Mr David Furnish. Similarly, Reinaldo Avila da Silva, the partner of Baron Mandelson of Foy, will continue to be known as such, and was not upgraded to 'Baroness' when they married in 2023.

Non-binary people

The 'Mx' prefix, pronounced 'mix', while very new to some, dates back to 1977 and is often used when someone doesn't wish to be identified by their gender – which is usually (but not always) because they identify as non-binary. Like 'Ms' is non-specific to marital status, 'Mx' is non-specific to gender. The 'x' was added to the 'M' so there is no confusion with the French honorific 'M', denoting 'Monsieur'. It is styled in writing as 'Mx Alex Taylor' and as 'Mx Taylor' in formal speech. It isn't difficult.

Married couples with different titles

When writing to a male / female couple who share the same surname but one has a professional or more significant title than the other, it is convention to still follow the 'man then woman' format. The titles and names are included as follows: 'Dr David and Mrs Moore' or 'Professor David and Mrs Moore'; 'Mr David and Dr Rosemary Moore' or 'Mr David and Dame Rosemary Moore'. But, as mentioned, it is hard to present an argument besides patriarchal convention as to why there is this insistence on putting the man's name first. If you want to invert it, giving rank to the professional or more significant title rather than the gender, then insert both first names. Therefore, 'Dr Rosemary and Mr David Turner'.

In an instance where the couple are both brainboxes and have the same clever title, they would be styled as 'Professor David and

Professor Rosemary Turner' or 'Dr David and Dr Rosemary Turner'. If preferred, this can be inverted – therefore, 'Professor Rosemary and Professor David Turner'.

Or, if you feel a bit grand and want to use a fairly extinct but still correct plural, 'the Doctors Turner' or 'the Professors Turner' are your friends.

Double-barrels and suffixes

Historically, double-barrelled surnames used to be quite smart, although usually only in play when a less illustrious man married a woman from a far grander family and they wanted to preserve the legacy rather than let it be lost in marriage. In such an instance, the more notable surname was placed last.

In the nineteenth century, the practice of hyphenation spread among the middle classes, with aspirational Brits thinking that double-barrelled surnames (so-called to evoke the purportedly gentlemanly pastime of hunting) would win them respect when moving about in society. This was most frequently seen with people with the commonplace surname 'Smith' who wanted to add a touch of class to the otherwise bland – so added a name, often that of their spouse, to create names such as 'Vernon-Smith'.

Today, double-barrelled names are seen more often and transgress any class connotations. Same-sex or different-sex couples might choose to double-barrel upon marriage, so neither loses their identity and their name strikes a more equal, contemporary note. While you do not have to use a hyphen for a double-barrelled name, it is often easier to use one so one name doesn't get lost when booking flights, hotels or the like. The exception, as noted earlier, is if you are in the upper house of the Houses of Parliament. They insist on the practice so a newly ennobled peer from a more humble origin does not get confused for someone from a more elevated background if the names could be carelessly combined.

Take former Labour minister George Brown – who, upon receiving a life peerage in 1970 Dissolution Honours List, wished to be styled 'Lord George Brown'. But the Garter King of Arms (the person who oversees titles, based at the College of Arms in London) argued that peerage titles traditionally include only surnames, not forenames. If Brown had got his way, people may have assumed he was the younger son of a duke, a marquess or an earl. Brown had no sympathy with the objection, however. Eventually, the Garter King of Arms gave way on the condition that Brown simultaneously change his surname to George-Brown, so finally his title ended up as Baron George-Brown of Jevington in the County of Sussex. A story of British stubbornness from both sides!

Americans rarely go in for double-barrelled surnames but do go in for suffixes after the last name such as Snr (Senior), Jnr (you cracked the code – Junior) and, confusingly, Roman numerals. In Britain, numerals are only ever affixed to sovereigns.* An alien who has just landed on a random street in a backwater, nondescript part of the US may be forgiven for thinking they have just settled inches away from the home of a great noble dynasty. Although, sadly for any alien tourists, Randy T. Hunter III is not the reigning monarch but an alligator farmer in the Kissimmee everglades.

---

* Boats and ships, on the other hand, use numbers instead of numerals. The longest reigning monarch is styled 'Queen Elizabeth II', whereas the now-decommissioned cruise liner is the *Queen Elizabeth 2*.

Save the dates

Did you know that a 'save the date' is not the actual invitation but a promise of one at a later stage? So many people think they need to reply to them. But STDs, as they are often called, only need to have the host's name, the date and nature of the event (and for whom, if different from the host) and vague location listed. For example, 'Luton, to celebrate Tom's thirtieth birthday, 1st February 2025'. You can send them up to a year in advance, although six to eight months is more usual unless you are asking guests to go international.

Guests don't need to formally reply to save the dates, although it's never a bad idea to make some excitable comment in passing or in text to the host. Guests can decline the invitation when it arrives, however, if the date no longer works – although they should understand why the host may be a bit put out. If the guest knows they can't come when they receive the STD, they should send a regretful message.

Anyone who is sent a save the date by the host should then get a proper invitation unless they wish to sever the friendship. Although this can be diplomatically tricky, hosts do not need to send all guests a save the date, only the key ones.

Nice stiff ones: Invitations

Britain loves a formal invitation. In Asia and the Middle East, all invitations are word of mouth or electronic, but living up to our bureaucratic tendencies as a nation, receiving a stiff card invitation (in less smutty times, called a 'stiffy') immediately elevates the event to give it more grandeur and importance than something fired off via WhatsApp. Imagine relegating the upcoming nuptials of a couple to the paperless post. While resorting to the online world is appropriate for some events, it isn't ideal for everything.

By whichever means hosts solicit the attendance of their guests, invitations must follow a certain format, containing all the relevant information a guest needs. If a guest has to ask the host something, the invitation has not served its full purpose.

An invitation should contain the answers to the following questions:

The Who – Who is the host?

The What – Is it a lunch? Dinner? Drinks reception? Wedding?

The Where – The location of the event, but only the top line of the venue's address. There's no need to state ungainly postcodes. You can stick those on the additional information sheets. For example, if you were being a bit posh getting married at The Ritz in London, you don't need to write 'The Ritz, 150 Piccadilly, London W1J 9BR'. You can simply state 'The Ritz, London' on the invitation and give more info elsewhere.

The When – It's usually helpful to put the date and start time on the invitation, too.

The RSVP – Usually, this is positioned in the bottom left-hand corner, and what you include indicates how you would want guests to reply – for example, a postal address, an email address, a telephone number or a combination of those options.

Design-wise, there is no one correct procedure or format other than making sure all the above information is included. Hosts can get creative if they want, allowing the invitation to be a preview of what the party will be like. A plain, off-white stiff invitation with a cursive font probably means it's going to be a grander or more formal affair than something in Barbie-pink with glitter in the envelope. (Incidentally, people who put glitter in envelopes should be sent to the Tower of London.)

The guests' names are written, by hand, in the top left-hand corner in black or blue ink. There was once an old-fashioned rule that only women wrote in blue ink. Hopefully, we have all matured as a society and realised that shouldn't be a thing.

In Britain, only the names written on the invitation are invited, either in the longer formal style or the now more usual casual. 'Mr and Mrs Peter Smith' would mean it is our good friends Peter and Jane who are invited and not their children, for example, as their names do not appear. In other countries, especially in the Far East, an invitation is to the entire family, named or otherwise, but British manners are much stricter on who is and isn't invited.

Should just one person be invited, but the host has extended them the courtesy of bringing a friend of their choosing (it's very down-market to call it a 'plus one'), the styling is 'Mr Peter Smith and guest'. The named invitee needs to let the host know who they will be bringing – and in this day and age, their dietary requirements – well in advance. The usual form is to do this in the written reply. Any guest that gets brought must be sure to get along with the host and the other guests. This is not an opportunity to bring someone's ex or sworn enemy for some drama.

Timeframes for invitations

With life more hectic than ever, the lead time for inviting people to events has changed from the standards set two to three decades ago.

There is a long-running half-joke that for those living in London, for anything more than a quick chai latte, you have to invite them at least eleven weeks in advance if you want to stand any chance of them being available, as their diaries fill up quicker than most.

For relaxed entertaining like dinner parties and candlelight suppers, hosts now usually text around their intended guest list to see if a specific date works; this is often done eight to ten weeks in advance. No actual physical invitation is sent, although it is prudent for hosts to send a text three weeks in advance to firm up the details such as arrival time, and to double-check any dietary requirements.

Wedding invitations are sent ten to twelve weeks in advance, although for weddings a save the date card or text should have been sent a few months before. The formal invitation just serves as the one to officially reply to and confirms the exact details.

Invitations for celebration events, such as anniversary parties or landmark birthdays, can be sent eight to ten weeks in advance – but again, an STD is usually issued beforehand to make sure enough people are able to come.

In British culture, formal invitations are not issued for funerals. Instead, mourners are told by word of mouth. This came as much surprise to one former American first lady, who let it be known that she wouldn't be attending the official funeral of a prominent British politician without being formally issued an invitation. As the private secretary in charge of the guest list retorted to his counterpart in the US, 'You don't get a stiffy for a stiffy.' A key tenet of British etiquette.

Wedding invitations

For many decades, British wedding invitations followed a very set formula, and they all looked the same. They were printed on white or cream card, with a portrait orientation, eight inches high by six across, and were folded like a greeting card. It was only on the front of the 'card' that the text was printed – always in an Edwardian Script–esque font.

Although this is now looked at as a colossal waste of paper, the thinking was that they could stand proudly on mantel shelves in the weeks leading up to the wedding. In reality, they were, in all likelihood, a hangover from a time before envelopes, which were invented in the late eighteenth century. Before envelopes, handwritten letters were written on a single sheet and folded; and as the modern printing press had yet to be invented, these letters were how invitations were issued, if they weren't issued instead by the local town crier. The formality of the folded sheet is a vestigial remnant of earlier forms of paper correspondence, and the cursive lettering is a throwback to handwriting.

Many couples getting married today wish to put their own spin on invitation design and opt for something unique – and often using less paper. While the smartest of British weddings may still stick to using the traditional form for design, it is much more acceptable to get creative, although those who do try to reinvent the wheel need to remember that an invitation has to contain all the pertinent facts, as noted above.

Traditionally, a bride's parents would be the 'hosts' of the wedding, and so invitations would come from them. Life is different now; many couples have both sets of parents contribute, and even contribute or pay for the wedding themselves. The conventional choice of wording is, if we're being honest, governed by the once-accepted custom that still-married parents were marrying off their natural daughter. From that form, listed in full below, all other formulations follow.

Mr and Mrs Peter Smith
request the pleasure of your company
at the marriage of their daughter
Georgiana
to
Mr George Armstrong
at St Giles's Church, Cormick Warren
on Saturday 4ᵗʰ April
at 2.30 o'clock
and afterwards at
The Cock and Trumpet

As with all invitations, in the bottom left are the RSVP details. Nothing is written in the bottom right, however, unless a revolution is in the air. Things like the dress code and any additional information is often written on a small enclosed additional sheet. The honorifics of the hosts ('Mr', 'Miss', and the like) can be left out to give a really modern feeling to a wedding invitation, but the exclusion of surnames is not wise, especially if the couple have slightly nondescript first names.

Every couple is different, but a good contemporary catch-all wording, one which my husband and I used for our own wedding, is as follows:

Mr George Armstrong and Miss Georgiana Smith
together with their families
request the pleasure of your company
at their marriage
at St Giles's Church, Cormick Warren
etc

This modern option is inclusive for all sides of the family, doesn't make a big thing out of who is supposedly footing the bill (which is irrelevant for guests), and puts the couple front and centre for the day. For those marrying later in life, or where no parents are still alive, the 'together with their families' bit can be deleted.

Sometimes I do feel sorry for my parents' generation, who were probably thrown weddings that their own parents wanted and thoroughly approved of – as they too were given weddings where everything was decided by their parents. Each generation sees the wedding of their children as 'their turn' to put on the wedding they wanted. That school of thought was maybe wiser back then, as people married when they were younger and less experienced than many people today, so it was a matter of practicality. This cycle has stopped, however, as pretty much everyone getting married now has existing ideas as to what they want and are determined to do it their way – even if someone else is paying for large parts of it. This, alas, often leads to conflict and tears on pillows. Communication, openness and the ability to compromise are the watchwords.

I could fill another book just with variations on the traditional form or alternatives to the 'together with their families' route. But whatever the wording a couple chooses, common sense should prevail. A wedding invitation should not look to replicate a Hollywood blockbuster poster, with multiple names all vying for position. This is especially true when there are split families and couples try to appease and include everyone. It looks ridiculous.

If a couple are insistent on creating a second or third class of wedding guest and inviting certain people only for the wedding breakfast or evening reception, an alternative type of invitation has to be printed with the following wording:

Mr George Armstrong and Miss Georgiana Smith
together with their families
request the pleasure of your company

at a reception following their marriage
on Saturday 4th April
at The Cock and Trumpet

This time, the arrival time is written in the bottom right-hand corner, and the RSVP is found in the bottom left-hand corner. For guests wondering whether they will be eating or just enjoying drinks, it should be very clear from the stated time. If it's four o'clock in the afternoon, it's highly likely they'll be enjoying the wedding breakfast. If it's half past seven in the evening, they should prepare themselves for a few glasses of Prosecco and, if they're lucky, something called 'bowl food'.

Whether it's to the whole shebang or just the after-party, guests' names should be handwritten in black or blue ink in the top left-hand corner. Depending on the formality of the occasion, they may be written in the full written form ('Mr Alex Brown') or – more frequently seen today – just the first names for an air of cosy familiarity ('Alex'). As with any type of invitation, if a name is not written, they are not invited. It is very poor form for parents to ask if their children are invited if the children's names are not written alongside their parents. It puts the hosts in a very difficult position of having to say no. Those getting married, however, should take a proactive approach. It is now not enough just not to name the children on the invitation. Somewhere on the additional information sheet there should be a cleverly worded, succinct phrase that outlines the child policy. Anything from a direct 'The wedding is for adults only' to the alarming 'Due to the large ponds and sequence of trap doors at the venue, we regret that children are not allowed'.

If the munchkin moratorium means the named guests have to decline the invitation, couples getting married usually, and quite easily, find ways to cope.

Replying to invitations

However you are invited, your reply must be sent within three to four days. You know full well whether you can (or want to) attend the moment you read the invitation. Leaving it longer than this and having to get the host to chase you is awkward and does not reflect well. Are you waiting for a better offer? In our busy lives, there is also a strong argument for getting it sorted before you forget.

When Facebook launched their events function however many years ago, they introduced this rather weird third option of the 'maybe attending', which I am sure was millennial code for 'I'm not coming but don't want to offend you by saying that, so we'll go through the motions of giving you faint hope I'll be there' – making it next to impossible to prepare the right number of vol-au-vents for the maybe-attending brigade.

As for how to reply, we shall begin with the formal style, which is still correct if a physical address is printed on the invitation under 'RSVP'. This means you send your acceptance or refusal by post, handwritten in the third person:

Mr and Mrs Oscar Allonby thank Mrs Richard Arbuthnot for her kind invitation to dinner on Friday 18th April and have much pleasure in accepting.

If an email address is printed, instead of or as well, I see no reason why the above style cannot be typed into the body of an email and sent. Quite grand and certainly memorable. You are repeating the name(s) of the guest(s), the host's name(s), thanking them, stating the date and type of party it is, and then saying yes or no. That's all you need to do. Keep it simple.

In the event a refusal has to be sent, the reply is largely the same, repeating your name, their name, the date and party type, but with a different ending:

Mr and Mrs Oscar Allonby thank Mrs Richard Arbuthnot for her kind invitation to dinner on Friday 18th April but regrettably are unable to accept.

There is no need for the actual reason you can't go to be stated in the reply, which should be a relief to those who decline things because they can't think of anything worse. Thus, adding things like '. . . due to having to attend a family celebration' or '. . . due to a work commitment' is incorrect. Of course, if it's your best friend inviting you, you may want to send a text or tell them in passing why you can't go, but for everyone else, less is more. This rule can apply to any invitation you are declining, whether formally or informally.

If you are allowed to bring a guest, ensure you name them in your reply, like so:

Mr Peter Smith and his guest, Miss Penelope Bristols, thank Mrs Richard Arbuthnot, etc.

It is bad form to change the guest at the last minute, although in the flaky culture we now live in, it will happen. A call should be placed post-haste in this circumstance, asking the host if it is okay to bring someone different – or not at all – now the original guest has been indisposed.

Wedding invitations today usually come with a reply card, as no one seems to know how to reply in the written form, and due to the expense and labyrinthine nuances of organising a modern wedding, it's helpful for hosts to get as many replies as they can sooner rather than later. All the guest has to do is write their name(s), tick whether they are attending or not attending, and state any dietary requirements. For those who do know the traditional third-person wording for replying to invitations, there is no need to show off and send one when a reply card is provided. Go with the flow!

Generous wedding hosts will have included a stamp on the reply card's envelope – they may as well make it as easy as possible for guests to reply promptly. There is, however, no need to source the correct postage for any guests coming from overseas.

As noted, many now choose paperless invitations and will use sites on the internet to issue their missives, all of which allow the recipients to hit one button or the other to say yay or nay. While the tech may be modern, the manners are not, and the same 'reply as soon as possible' rule applies.

Once a guest has accepted an invitation, whatever the form, there's no turning back. Failing to turn up is simply not done unless you come down with a highly contagious illness like Ebola, or perhaps have to leave the country to stay one step ahead of an extraordinary rendition to Guantanamo. Those who do perform an attendance U-turn should make sure their excuse is a good one, offer profuse apologies and mean them. Sending a handwritten letter of apology isn't a bad idea either, as well as a bouquet of flowers the day of the party itself so you can be there in spirit and in buds.

The telephone

It was a Brit who invented the telephone (Alexander Graham Bell), and the first telephone call was made from Brown's Hotel in London. Therefore, Brits are right to have a sense of ownership of the telephone and the accompanying manners.

When telephones were installed in private residences, no one knew how to use the new device properly – shouting down it, unaware of how it all worked and how their voice was being transported to the person on the other end. Telephone directories of the time had etiquette guides at the back to advise people on how to behave when placing a call; the word 'hello' was encouraged by Thomas Edison as *the* way to answer a phone. (His rival, Bell, preferred 'ahoy'.)

Everything being cyclical, shouting down the telephone returned with the rise of the mobile phone. Cast your mind back to Dom Joly's 'I'M ON THE TRAIN' character from *Trigger Happy TV*. Thankfully, probably due to Joly's satire and common sense, we've finessed that irritating habit out of common practice, and most mobile phone users are aware that you can whisper down the phone and still be heard by whoever is on the other end.

We all know someone who has a telephone voice – many of us may have one ourselves, too. In the world before caller ID, I would rather grandly answer my parents' landline with 'Hello, who's speaking please?' which I felt set the right tone, even if I was still in short trousers. It was a relief to my parents I didn't opt to answer 'Mayfair, 482'. (Which was just as well, given we lived in Bristol.)

Telephone voices, although good for gentle teasing, were probably born of necessity, as people had to speak slightly slower than normal conversation and – in the days before Wi-Fi calling and better signal – enunciate carefully to ensure the person on the other end understood what was being said. There were also a great deal of aspirational answerers wanting to elevate their establishment in the mind of the caller by speaking with a slightly 'posher' voice.

Today, it's highly likely we know exactly who is calling, as telephones flash up with names or numbers and even photographs of the person buzzing you; so, use their name ('Hello, Zennor') when answering. It's important to save people's numbers on your phone, or else when you give a more generic 'Hello' they could be offended you have not saved their details.

Millennials and Gen Zers are averse to using the telephone. If a call comes through on their mobile, they will automatically assume nuclear war has just broken out and they need to prepare for the worst. It's much safer and nicer for them to send a text or voice message.

Voice notes are the new frontier of telephone communication, although – as the often-quoted meme says – there's a difference between a quick voice note to someone and sending them a pod-cast's worth of audio. Being succinct is an art when it comes to voice notes. To best achieve this, resist the great urge (and I'm par-ticularly looking at the shyer amongst us) to send one as you go about your errands, just to fill the void of having no one to talk to, text or interact with. It is fine to be alone with your thoughts – no one is looking at you as you walk down the street thinking you are so boring not to be with anyone.

Once a voice note has been sent, adding a line of text afterwards to summarise the contents of the oratory is a consideration few do, but a habit that should be encouraged. That way, the recipient knows if you need something urgently or are just passing the time of day as you mince down the road.

I am always baffled when I'm walking around London (though I've seen it all over the world) by the rise of public video calls. You see people from all walks of life who have decided that the other person needs to see them going about their business, all viewed from the most unflattering angle, looking up under the chin. Just because the technology exists to make video calls, it doesn't mean that all calls need to be on video. Keep them for when you are static and in a private or semi-private space. Similarly, making phone calls using the speaker-phone function in public is a gross breach of good manners. Filthy looks can be shot in the direction of the miscreant.

Greeting cards

Britain is a country that loves the written form, and while letter-writing may be all but gone, we do still keep the practice up by writing and sending greeting cards, especially around birthdays and Christmas. Fastidious senders of cards will keep a perennial calendar – or 'birthday book' – to hand, reminding them of dates for their nearest and dearest, checking it at the start of each week to see who needs a card.

Inscriptions for birthday cards do not need to be long. Many Brits prefer a witty one-liner over padded prose of actual sentiment. If sending cards a few days in advance, you can write the birthday date in a corner on the back of the envelope so the recipient knows it is not to be opened until the day itself. Oversized cards are never correct, and ones with saccharine sentiments such as 'To my darling husband' or 'For a special daughter' don't sit well with the traditionally cynical British psyche.

If someone misses marking your birthday with a card or message once, it is not an issue. If they miss it twice, it is still forgivable. But three times, and it means they probably hate you.

Invented by accident by Sir Henry Cole in 1840 and then made commercial in 1843, Christmas cards are still popular, although the number I receive each year is dropping, and I suspect in fifteen years the practice will be obsolete. While historically they were all opened on Christmas Day, they are now usually sent in the first couple of weeks of December and opened upon receipt.

It is important to write the names of all recipients in the card. Don't just sign off with your names, failing to personalise it. While some who do this may think it shows quite how many cards they have to send (omitting recipient names supposedly saves time), it totally defeats the purpose of showing people you are thinking of them at Christmas. You may as well just not bother.

Those who enclose round-robin family newsletters (which invariably only boast about the wonderful things the family has been up to in the past year, failing to mention any negatives) are unaware that everyone else reads them while cringing at the immodesty.

Those with birthday books probably also have Christmas card lists. A mildly threatening British idiom often heard is 'I'll remove you from my Christmas card list'. For most, this will be an expression and nothing else. For some, however, it is an actual actionable threat. Such lists are to remind the sender who they need to send cards to and who sent them cards in previous years. I have a rule that if you haven't sent us a card for three consecutive years, you are off our Christmas card list. You have to give to receive – that's always been my motto.

Design-wise, Christmas cards can be of any festive scene, although the smartest cards show something religious or are a wintery Old Master painting. Growing up, there was much uproar when my parents chose a cartoony image of ice-skating nuns. It is still tattooed on my mind. Beaming family portraits are probably best left to members of the Royal Family and the prime minister, rather than their subjects.

Depending on who is in your address book, you may even opt for a card that reads 'Festive greetings' instead of 'Happy Christmas'. While it sounds slightly clinical, it is more inclusive.

Stamps

Stamps bearing the King's face should always be used on private letters and greeting cards, affixed to the top right-hand corner of the envelope. As tempting as it may be to take your personal letters to the office franking machine and get your employer to subsidise you, please resist the urge. Not only is it a touch immoral, but the presence of a franking mark on a handwritten envelope drains it of any style.

Brits being how we are, with our inherent never-questioned love for the monarchy, have even applied our treason laws to stamps. Affixing a stamp bearing the monarch's image upside down is officially known as 'postal regicide'. This is one of the most severe and heinous criminal acts a British citizen can do, carrying with it the highest – and most justified – of penalties.

The Royal Mail is the finest postal service in the world (which gives you a rough idea of how good they are elsewhere) and will check each letter for the alignment of the stamp. When they spot any clear examples of postal regicide, they will open the letter to find the sender's address. The data is handed over, pretty damn quickly, to a member of the security services, who then despatch a hit squad to the sender's address, arresting and charging them under the 1848 Treason Felony Act. The current penalties are a life sentence for a second-class stamp and an automatic death penalty for a first-class stamp. Stamps for overseas post will get you sent to The Hague for the International Criminal Court's consideration.

While these crimes and punishments may or may not be genuine, it is still best practice to not stick any stamp upside down.

Letters

With the exception of thank yous and condolences, most other forms of letter are now typed. The Royal Household, however, retains the charming yet time-consuming practice that any letter sent to the King or Queen will be replied to by one of the correspondence team. A record is kept by Buckingham Palace of who has sent what and which stock reply they were sent last time, to ensure the exact same reply is not sent again. Even if insults or words that are worlds removed from the usual language of the court are used in the original letters, each will receive a polite reply in due course from the Palace. Always better to be the bigger person and turn the other cheek.

With more people saving their wrists for other categories of activity, the advice that will follow here on letters relates to official correspondence in the world of work. For those who wish to employ their flexor carpi radialis for untyped letters, the rules here are transferable.

The classic opening to a letter is to use 'Dear' – which, way back when, was a sign of endearment. A word of warning to speakers of English as a foreign language: please be under no such illusion that just because a letter (or email) starts with 'Dear', we hold the recipient in any high regard. Whether we are complaining about a missed bin collection or writing a final missive to a much-loved dying great-aunt, Brits will start the letter the same way, which may be misleading.

It is always best to know to whom you are writing before you begin. Sounds simple enough, but there is still a worrying case of the 'Dear Sirs' or the 'To whom it may concerns'. Every effort should be made to find the name of a specific person before a letter

is sent. With search engines and online CVs now widely accessible, it is easier than ever before to source a name. Failing that,
there is always the telephone and calling the local council, or wherever you are writing, and asking for the identity of the deputy
assistant vice-head of paperclips.

The practice of starting a letter with just 'Sir', which was only used
by men when writing to someone they did not know at all, is totally extinct now, except for when people write to a British national
newspaper.

'Dear Mr Smith' or 'Dear Ms Jones' is perfectly acceptable when
you do not know the person, or don't know them well enough to
use their first name. It is always best, as with much of British etiquette, to begin more conservatively and then adjust downwards.
Remember that familiarity breeds contempt. While some may not
see the need for addressing them formally, they will not think badly
of the sender; whereas someone who does not feel you have
earned the right to use their first name yet will take great umbrage
at the liberty, rendering any chance of the contents of your letter
being given the desired attention.

If you have used the formal styling of a person's name to open
your letter, it closes with 'Yours sincerely'. (If you do have to write
a letter without a specific name at the top – 'Dear Sir', for example –
the sign-off is 'Yours faithfully'.) When letters begin with the more
relaxed 'Dear Jane', the closing can be warmed up to include something less official. There is no one-size-fits-all here; each sender can
use whatever they feel is appropriate. 'With every best wish' or
'Only good wishes' are personal favourites, but creativity can be
applied. If you are susceptible to flamboyant tendencies, the late
Noël Coward's letters are a good font of inspiration for more interesting sign-offs: 'All love and hugs', 'Your affectionate, but regal',
'The quaintest of quaints' and 'Love, love, love'.

Letters of condolence

Brits have a funny relationship with death. Granny would get very cross with people who dared comfort her after my grandfather died. 'I haven't lost David, he's died!' she'd say. In more correct British speak, euphemistic talk – especially around death – is not encouraged. Spade-a-spade and all that.

Aside from 'people's princesses', we don't usually go in for histrionic wailing, preferring some stifled sniffles and silent tears instead. It may not be as effective as the mourning styles of the continentals, but it keeps the British therapy industry alive.

Growing up, I noticed my own wonderful father would always turn to the obituary section of the newspaper first, to see who had died and if he knew any names. A morbid habit that has, like so much of life, been replaced by reading posts online about who has died. As with announcing an engagement, all close family and friends should be told of the death before any announcement, printed or digital, is issued.

Many people have said that in a time of grieving, a sympathy letter from friends of the deceased has helped temper the grief. But many people, especially emotion-averse Brits, can struggle with knowing how to write one. Such letters (never emails or texts) should be sent out as soon as possible after hearing of the death, and usually go to the next of kin. If your friend's father died, however, and the next of kin is the deceased's wife, then write to both your friend (the deceased's child) and the next of kin (the wife). In such an instance, make sure you say who you are in your letter to the next of kin if you are unsure if they will know.

The contents of your letter must come from the heart. Phoney sentiment will stand out, especially to British ears – although writing from the heart and not the head is not a British speciality, especially for the less emotional older generations. Remember, however, that letters of condolence are mainly to comfort the bereaved. Say one or two positive things about the deceased, but the rest should be directed at the recipient. If you offer to help, then make sure you mean it.

Condolence letters, which should ideally be written on social correspondence paper, are also a good means of saying whether you will be at the funeral. If you cannot attend, then, just as with responses to everyday invitations, you do not need to state why.

Although years ago, to send an 'In sympathy' card would have been tantamount to poor taste – what was known as a Hallmark approach to mourning – their use is now much more widespread, and can be useful if you did not know the deceased well enough to write a full letter but wish to show your sympathy to the bereaved.

Do not write a condolence letter or send any card if a death notice has been printed in a newspaper or issued elsewhere instructing that the next of kin is not receiving letters at this time.

If you are sadly the one grieving and receive such letters, they do not need to be replied to in any form until after the funeral.

Thank-you letters

While evidence of handwritten gratitude is few and far between these days, saying thank you will never be out of fashion. A thank-you *letter* is always preferable, but a grateful text or phone call is much better than a rude silence.

Diana, Princess of Wales, would reportedly begin her thank-you letter before she left for a dinner, writing the salutation and a fairly generic opening sentence ('Dear Carolyn, What a truly delicious evening we all had . . .') and then finishing it once she returned home, and posting it the next day.

But the best case for bothering to write such letters comes from my friend Daphne, with whom I used to stay while I was working in London but living in Manchester. She let me stay in one of the bedrooms in her beautiful *Mary Poppins*-esque Chelsea town-house, and the first time I met her, she told me this story.

Daphne and her sister grew up in Cheshire, and every Christmas they would each receive a crisp £1 note from their father's cousin. Once they reached an age where they could put pen to paper, they would each write a thank-you letter to their cousin once removed. Good manners still prohibit people from talking about a woman's age, but to give some context here, let me say that Daphne and her sister were born in the reign of Edward VIII, so a £1 note for children was a heck of a lot of money. A big reason to be grateful!

There was some family feud with this relative, so the girls never met her, nor knew the reason why the relative was exiled. But still, each Christmas, the two £1 notes would arrive, and the sisters would write their respective letters. Skipping forward a few years, Daphne was working, and the value of a £1 note decreased with each year. But still, the money and thank-you letters were sent. Not too fussed about family politics, Daphne and her sister added in a line to their notes that they'd love to finally meet the estranged relative and didn't care about whatever had happened in the past. They never got a reply. But the next Christmas, like clockwork, the money was sent to each sister.

Now in their mid-thirties, Daphne's sister announced she would stop writing to thank their benefactor as their repeated pleas to meet were always ignored, and the pound note was now a bit laughable to give two grown working women. Maybe if they stopped writing, the money would stop, and the relative would get the hint. But Daphne decided to keep writing regardless. And still, for a few more years, both sisters were sent the £1.

Then, one Christmas, nothing; neither sister received the ritualistic pound note. Shortly after, Daphne received a letter telling her that her father's cousin had died a few weeks ago, and in her will was an extraordinary, life-changing amount of money. It had been left to Daphne, because Daphne always wrote a thank-you letter. The sister wasn't left anything. With some of that money, Daphne was able to buy her beautiful Chelsea townhouse, where I always adored staying and, on occasion, pretending it was my own! And having been told that story, you can bet that every time I stayed with Daphne, I sent a thank-you letter. (You never know.)

The old rule used to be that for a weekend stay, you wrote two sides of paper (ideally two separate sheets, not writing on the back), but for a dinner or a present, you only had to write one side. Today, any length is better than no length, but do take from the old rule that for greater displays of hospitality, you may need to show greater levels of gratitude. The old rule of only writing to the hostess when thanking for hospitality is obsolete with a change in gender norms and marital roles.

Thank-you letters should be sent as quickly as possible, although for letters thanking someone for Christmas presents, it is okay to send them the first week of January, after any festive and New Year celebrations have concluded. Birthday present thanks, however, should be sent within a few days; one for a dinner or similar should be posted the next day. But a late thank-you letter is better than no thank-you letter at all.

Emails

While email is distinctly less formal and more efficient, it is still a form of mail, and many of the customs and mechanics have their etymology in the world of letter-writing. CC (carbon copy) of course stems from when a sheet of carbon paper was placed in between two sheets of regular paper in a typewriter to produce a duplicate.

Many fall into the trap of thinking that as email is quicker, they can shed formalities, mistaking courtesies for some sort of restrictive skin. For Brits, it is again much better to start off observing them and then relax as you get to know someone. Email me with a 'Hi Will' when we've never met and I don't know who you are, and you'll be sent straight to the Siberia that is my spam ('spam' is what Brits call 'junk mail'). 'Dear Mr Hanson' is preferable, but 'Dear William (if I may?)' is passable. (The 'yours faithfully/sincerely' rules for letters are the same for emails, too.)

While I am all for people being polite and acutely aware of their actions and how they affect others, Brits do have a tendency to take this too far when writing emails. As tone and body language are not seen, they cannot offset any overt over-niceness. Humble writing, which relies heavily on what are known as qualifiers, is used too often. The advice to Brits or anyone with over-polite inclinations: avoid, where possible.

Qualifiers are words such as 'actually', 'just', 'sorry', 'probably', 'sort of' and 'perhaps'. Take this sentence, which, for many Brits reading it, will be a typical sentence seen in workplaces across the nation:

Sorry to bother you – I'm just emailing to ask whether you can perhaps send me the proposal, please.

For any writing away from the world of work, there is nothing wrong with using any of these qualifiers in moderation, but for direct and efficient communication, emailers are better placed to strip them from their requests and e-missives.

Let's try that sentence again:

I'm emailing to ask whether you can send me the proposal, please.

All qualifiers have been removed, as has the apology at the start. If the recipient hasn't sent you the proposal when you asked for it or were told it would be with you, you don't need to fall into the British trap of apologising. They could have communicated with you that it would be slipping into your inbox later than advertised – and they chose not to. Or they forgot. *You* have nothing to be sorry for, even though the apology comes from a good place. It's a British reflex we need to train ourselves out of doing in this context. Just as walking up to a group of new people and saying 'sorry for interrupting' is a bad idea as it alerts them to the fact you're interrupting, the same principle applies to your emailing. (Non-Brits, however, should be wary that when the fault lies with them, and a Brit says sorry in an email, it's highly likely they don't mean it.)

The qualifier 'just' is the most commonly seen. You aren't just doing anything. You are either doing it or you are not. Take ownership of your actions. These words dilute your message and can make the writer seem weak. When emailing B2B (Brit to Brit), it is fine – we understand the code and the fact the sender has spent two hours worrying about being too direct – but when communicating with other nationalities, it puts us at a disadvantage.

Our nation's inbuilt Olympic-standard small-talk abilities extend, more or less, to emails, too. The body of most emails from Brits, unless to a very close friend or colleague, will begin with 'I hope this email finds you well' or 'Hope you are keeping dry in all this horrid rain' (or similar). Going straight into the main thrust of the email is alarmingly direct for us, and likely to make us feel we're being reprimanded. Adding some meaningless cushioning to each end of the email is standard practice.

A way to elevate the small talk for emails, however, is to personalise it to the recipient. There should really not be much need to use the 'I hope this email finds you well' line once any level of rapport has been established. You can look back over previous emails to find inspiration. Were they moving offices six months ago? Why not ask them if they have settled in okay or if they are missing the old place? Did you see on LinkedIn that their company has just announced a great new client? Why not mention that? While small talk in emails is useful for Brits, it doesn't need to be mundane.

Now, pay attention, non-Brits. Unless the Brit you are emailing is freelance, do not expect any reply to your message until the next working day. If you emailed them on a Saturday, you won't get a response until Monday at the earliest. This can lead to some frustration, especially for Americans and those living in countries with a harder work ethic than in Britain.

A few years ago, I was going to be spending a Monday morning doing a photo shoot for a newspaper with Myka Meier, my friend and colleague from New York. The location was a well-known five-star hotel in central London. The journalist from New York had loosely arranged everything with the hotel's PR department but had not got any written confirmation, and had mistakenly thought they could leave it until Saturday or Sunday to dot the i's and cross the t's. The American journalist soon realised this was a mistake as the British PR was not replying to emails and their work phone had been switched off. It was a weekend. Had we been in New York City, of course, emails and work calls would have been replied to. The stress this caused was interesting to observe, especially when the hotel PR glided in to greet us on the appointed Monday, totally unaware of the cross-cultural difference and the drama it had created.

Since 2017, our nearest neighbour, France, has had a law that protects employees from having to answer emails and respond to orders from superiors outside of office hours. The *droit à la déconnexion* (right to disconnect) means, in essence, if an employee doesn't react to a direct request outside of their contracted hours, they cannot in any way be penalised. Excessive legislation? Another excuse for the French not to do any work? You can make your own mind up. But while it probably is somewhat of an overreach, perhaps they have *un point*.

With email now the main form of work communication, the onus should be on the sender to respect the recipient's time, as Victoria Turk writes in *Digital Etiquette*. This is especially true if you are writing with a request or wish for your email to be viewed favourably. Are you asking the person you once did business with for some free advice for your daughter who's trying to get into the coffee-pod industry herself? Maybe don't send it at 9 a.m. on a Monday when there are more pressing matters and the weekend's email backlog to clear. Similarly, prepare to be universally loathed if you ask a supplier or client to do something major at 4.45 p.m. on a Friday.

While you may think you're being gloriously efficient to sit at your desk at 6 a.m., firing off emails left, right and centre as the morning coffee takes hold, your less productive colleagues are probably going to hate you when they check their inbox at 8 a.m. and are already drowning in your morning's fecundity.

This is where email scheduling comes in handy. A more recent innovation from most email applications, the 'schedule send' function allows you to pick a date and time for an email to be sent, allowing it to gracefully appear at a more sociable time. If you are emailing colleagues in vastly different time zones, of course, there is no issue with sending it early for you but a normal time for them.

While I don't want to do too much more America-bashing, it is always frustrating for Brits and other non-Americans to be given telephone numbers for their US-based chum without the international dialling code already affixed. Most of us, due to America's dominance, probably know that we have to add +1 to the number, but it still rankles when the courtesy is not there when they share it. Do they really expect that their number will work in other countries with no dialling code? That all our phone lines are connected without any form of telephonic bridge? Actually, don't answer that. With business so diverse and multinational, make sure you think globally when emailing.

CHAPTER SEVEN

Stand on the Right; Walk on the Left

In the ever-evolving tapestry of British life, where tradition meets the incessant buzz of modernity, the public arena remains a battleground of manners, a veritable coliseum where the gladiators of politeness cross swords with the barbarians of boorishness. As we step into the hallowed grounds of bars, pubs, shops and restaurants, the air thick with the scent of ale, commerce, culinary delights and the faintest hint of desperation, it behoves us to arm ourselves not with sword and shield, but with the more formidable weapons of etiquette and good grace.

In these arenas, the unwritten rules of conduct are as crucial as the regal legal tender that greases the wheels of commerce and conviviality. Here, amidst the unfortunate sound of clinking glasses and sizzling kitchens, the cacophony of bargain hunters and the symphony of social intercourse, the well-mannered individual shines like a beacon of hope in a sea of chaos. They navigate these waters with the ease of a seasoned sailor, their actions a ballet of politeness, their words a movement of civility, their very presence a testament to the enduring power of good manners.

Our common courtesies are perhaps even more important when in public, as we are on display to other people. People who are strangers to us. A large majority of us will care deeply about what other people think and how our actions are judged by those around us – even though we are, in all probability, never going to see any of them again. Some people, woe is us, just don't care and become irritable, inconsiderate and insolent when going about daily life.

As we embark on this journey through some of the most frequently patronised public spaces of Britain, let us don the heavy armour of patience, wield the shield of tolerance and brandish our swords of kindness. For in the grand scheme of things, it is not the battles we win or lose that define us, but the manner in which we fight them.

Queuing

For many people, if one single act summarises British manners, it is the queue. As George Mikes noted, 'An Englishman, even if he is alone, forms an orderly queue of one.'

Perhaps our education system is where many of us get our knack for queuing patiently. At my school we certainly spent a good whack of our time standing and waiting outside classrooms, the lunch hall, in the playground, and at the door at going-home time. One wonders whether we would have been any more academically gifted if we had spent just half of our queuing time in our classroom chairs.

But in Britain, no academic plaudit is as meritorious as being able to dutifully wait in a line. Despite the three funerals and constant stream of eulogies Queen Elizabeth II received upon her death in 2022, arguably the most fitting and poignant tribute from her subjects was the quarter of a million people who (with one or two exceptions) formed an orderly queue to see her lying in state at Westminster Hall.

We Brits are known for our orderly queuing behaviour due to our sustained cultural emphasis on politeness, respect for others and adherence to social norms – as has probably already become apparent in this book. Queuing is a way to maintain order and fairness in everyday interactions. It is often seen as a reflection of a society's values, and in the case of us Brits, it is a symbol of civility and consideration for others.

The beauty of a queue (and I am, of course, heavily biased here as both a Brit and an advocate for manners and etiquette) is that it is so elegantly fair. Participation in any queue shows that those in it have accepted the silent social contract that whoever arrived first goes first, rather than the person who is most able to elbow their way to the front of the scrum. Even where there is an unstructured queue, such as when ordering drinks at a bar, Brits have an uncanny antenna for knowing who was there before and when our turn is.

Americans, to give them credit, are also very good at 'standing in line', as they call it, whereas our European friends do lack this skill. Local guests at Disneyland Paris may be enjoying America's most popular export but have not learned anything from their British or American contemporaries. And don't get me started on the queuing behaviour at Disneyland Shanghai, which I visited while in China for work in 2018. Their lack of adherence to the usual rules of the queue gave rise to my British friend Kit and me blocking each of the queue-jumpers, all of whom waved vaguely into the middle distance and protested they were meeting their friend up ahead. Not on our watch. Our policing of the line turned out to be more thrill-inducing than the Voyage to the Crystal Grotto.

The temporary and fleeting nature of queues makes it hard for any scholar to trace their exact origins, but it is thought that certain historical events in our nation's history shaped how we queue and our reputation for being so good at it. A key moment in time was the Industrial Revolution.

'The orderly queue seems to have been an established social form in the early nineteenth century, a product of more urbanised, industrial societies which brought masses of people together,' says Dr Joe Moran, the author of *Queuing for Beginners: The Story of Daily Life from Breakfast to Bedtime*. With the dawn of proper shops, there was a move from the casual barter system seen at market stalls to the structure of a queue.

Where Britain's reputation as Olympic-standard, gold-medallist queuers was really won, however, was during the Second World War. Scholars note that the war propaganda was heavily reliant on British citizens doing their duty and taking turns. Queues became loaded with meaning, subtly drawing upon notions of decency, fair play and democracy (unlike the people we were fighting); and the now-ingrained reputation of the British as patient queuers was welded into our minds and those of the rest of the world.

I have a slightly different take, having enjoyed my fair share of queuing around the world. Brits *are* good at the art of the queue, but we are by no means perfect, especially in our now time-poor lives. It's just that every other nation is so very bad at queuing.

Pavement politesse

The majority of British pedestrians still demonstrate an impressive amount of courtesy and awareness of other people's personal space.

When in public, on a pavement or otherwise, Brits do not like loud, disruptive displays of bacchanalia. The pavement is a public, shared space, and anything that makes others assume you are not playing the game of considering those around you will irritate them.

When in a large group, do not walk in a horizontal line, blocking the passage of others. Instead, shatter into smaller groups of two or three if it's a wide pavement – and carry on walking. If there are many other people heading straight towards you and the pavement is too narrow to fit you all in, it is polite to stop and let the other people pass. Automatically assuming they are more important than you is healthy, and a good way to lead a mannerly life. (Hopefully they stop for you, too, leading to both polite parties giving small chuckles as to how courteous you have all been and how you have succeeded as humans.) Regardless of how many are in your party, pedestrians are advised to walk in as straight a line as possible when on the streets, rather than slaloming around, getting in everyone's way.

Note for visitors to Britain: when at a pedestrian crossing, you will be standing there an awfully long time if you have not pressed the button to cross. While some countries don't have the button system, we do, and it's both amusing and aggravating to join a group of people waiting for the lights to change only to find they haven't pressed the button.

Some rules of the pavement, however, have nearly been abandoned; this is perhaps understandable, seeing as these rules were created out of necessity hundreds of years ago. Back then, a gentleman would walk on the outside of the pavement, protecting the hopeless and hapless woman he was walking with from any nasty mud or water splashes from passing stagecoaches on the road. With a shift in gender norms and expectations, this rule can be used in moderation and depends on your company. If you know the person you are with will like your supposed protection, position yourself on the outside of the pavement as subtly as possible. No need to make a meal out of it or look for praise.

When going about your daily life solo, it is always best not to rush or hurry. You want to give the graceful appearance of being in control and at one with your day's schedule and priorities – even if, mentally, your brain is in overdrive with executive stress. Imagine a swan: graceful on the surface but, hidden beneath the water, flapping frantically.

Going down! Lifts and stairs

While the use of lifts (which are only called 'elevators' in the United States) is not exclusive to Britain, the way in which we use them is distinctly polite. But before that, a recap of the global rules on lift etiquette, including some modifications for the modern age . . .

Traditionally, in social settings, deference was given to women and older people. (If you were an old woman, then you were twice in luck.) Once the lift doors opened, in would walk the 'most important person' before anyone else. Today, it is better to avoid gender and try to focus on age, when possible.

Professionally, as we know, gender and age are irrelevant. Instead, we look to professional relationships to define who is senior: higher-ranked colleagues are 'more important' and clients are even 'more important' and should enter first. This rule still applies today in the workplace.

When the lift reaches its destination, the person who is closest to the lift door exits first. Nine times out of ten, unless a Viennese waltz has been attempted while journeying along the shaft, this will be the person who entered last – the junior. It frustrates me no end in hotels, where the receptionist or porter showing you to your room at check-in insists on you, the client, leaving the lift first so that you need to awkwardly brush past them and then have no idea which way to turn once in the corridor.

Regardless of who gets in and out first, once travelling up or down, absolute silence must be maintained unless you know all parties around you. Brits will avoid making eye contact with those in the lift, looking away sheepishly if it is established by accident. When a new person enters the lift during the course of the short journey, it is permitted to greet them, but – again – silently, with a slight nod or a tight-lipped smile. Speak at your peril.

Of course, those sadistic few who walk amongst us Brits can play on this long-established code of behaviour. The actress and infamous provocateur Miriam Margolyes recently got in a lift at BBC Broadcasting House with a young researcher who was escorting her back to reception after an interview. The lift only made it one floor before it opened and filled with BBC staff. The journey resumed in glacial silence until Miriam turned to the researcher and slowly and loudly asked, 'Wasn't Steve Coogan good as Jimmy Savile in that programme?' Right there and then, the poor chap wanted to die.

The rule of silence and an acute awareness of space may be more prevalent in Britain as, due to the heritage and history of many of our buildings, lifts tend to be much smaller and pokier than their counterparts in newer and bigger countries like America.

British staircases are, again, often not as grand as in other countries, unless in a palace or a grand house, and a code of behaviour applies to how we ascend and descend them. The more important person goes up the staircase first, but goes down the staircase last, following the junior. (Again, you can apply whichever methodology you wish as to how you define who the more important person in your party is.) The idea behind this is safety and dates back to a medieval code of chivalry. If a lady fell when walking up a set of stairs, the man behind her was there to cushion her fall, and he sustained the injuries. Similarly, when going down, the man would be in front to act as a courtly crash barrier.

These rules are applied today, although many will take issue with the rule about ascending stairs, citing men possibly looking up a woman's skirt, or just at any person's bottom. (The skirt thing was not an issue, of course, in the Middle Ages, when dresses were much longer.) If the staircase is wide enough, the two people ascending it can walk up more or less side by side, even if at a slight diagonal. But for narrower *escaliers*, try to stagger your ascension – and there is no delicate way to say this – so you don't have your face right behind their bum.

The London Underground

Britain proudly boasts the world's oldest underground railway, which is formally called the London Underground but colloquially called 'the tube'.

As with so much in British life, a strict code of behaviour – until now, uncodified in writing – has developed to guide the tube's 1.35 billion annual passengers in how to behave while using its labyrinthine network of tunnels and stations. It is very easy to spot a newcomer to the tube, their virgin status either because they have just moved to London from elsewhere in the UK or because they are visiting from another country.

There are, of course, many other cities around the world with subterranean transportation systems – New York's subway makes the Central line look like the Orient Express – and some in Asia are even more complicated than ours. But what sets the London Underground apart from all the others is the rules that passengers are expected to follow.* For those who break these rules, especially during busy commuting periods, be prepared to experience the spine-tingling wrath of a British tut.

Underground ingénues are marked out by waiting for the ticket barriers to close before tapping their payment card on the Oyster pad, inconveniencing the passengers behind them. Be a pro and know that so long as the LED has gone orange, you can tap away, regardless of the position of the barriers.

Next, when using the lengthy escalators, know that if you do not follow the clearly signposted 'stand on the right, walk on the left' rule, you will be considered one level down from a serial killer. In the 2014 film *Paddington*, the titular bear was confused when he saw a sign instructing 'Dogs must be carried', forcing the polite Peruvian to dog-nap the nearest available canine before he could use the escalator. Note that this only applies if you are with your own pet. Dogs are not mandatory.

Once on board, only talk to people you know in hushed tones . . . but not when it's crowded and you are pressed up against others – they will be able to hear every syllable. This is the same principle as lifts.

Do not eat anything smelly. Ideally, nothing bigger or more potent than a breath mint. If you even think about tucking into a lamb balti, regardless of whether the train is busy, Londoners will think

---

* Only the MRT in Singapore rivals the standards of behaviour of the London tube. There, friendly signs are displayed throughout the stations and carriages, offering buoyant mannerly advice in the form of rhyming couplets: 'Bag on the floor, there's room for more', 'Please be sweet and give up your seat' and the more alarming 'If you molest, we will arrest'.

very poorly of you indeed and may, if they can, move away. Public transportation is not the most hygienic of places, so you really will be playing fast and loose with your microbiome if you dare eat anything.

Only make eye contact with people you don't know if there's some minor drama – an overkeen busker, a drunk or an argument between other passengers. Unless such an instance occurs, the floor, your telephone and the overhead adverts for sending money abroad are the only acceptable places to stare.

Music, videos and podcasts are to be enjoyed only with your head-phones. The same goes for all calls, video or audio. The tube is not your own personal space, and how you behave in the privacy of your own home has to be left there when you are on board the carriage.

During busy periods, mind your baggage. Backpacks should be held in front of you, rather than worn conventionally, and bags should definitely not be placed on empty seats. Place it on your lap or the floor.

Especially during commuting times, do not be afraid to move down inside the carriage rather than standing around the doors, unless you are travelling just one stop. If you plan to ride it for a decent amount of time, scooch on down, please.

Stopping the doors from closing so your friend can catch up and join you does not make you a hero, it makes you a pillock of the highest order. We all think you're a nit and there is no elegant way to recover your modesty. There is usually always a train shortly behind the one you're holding up with your kamikaze routine. Although, that said, if the information board shows a train is six minutes away, know that, using the maths of a Londoner, this is the equivalent of an hour.

Style in the aisles: Supermarket manners

Very rarely in shops do we get to see a special offer on good manners. Instead, often on the hunt for bargains, consumers have spectacular lapses in common sense, leaving staff and other customers short-changed in the currency of civility. It didn't used to be like this. Before the arrival of supermarkets in Britain in 1948, shoppers individually visited the relevant shop that sold the commodity they required. With an elegant gesture to the items they needed, the shop assistant would weigh out exactly how much was requested before ringing up the price on the till. The customer never handled the goods on display. Shopping for groceries today is very different.

Most Brits appreciate the cheapness and convenience of our now beloved supermarkets (not surprisingly, we've even created a class system for them). But many find themselves on retail autopilot, performing actions and making choices that are so ingrained and routine that they rarely pause to think about them and the consequences. Supermarkets, like any shop, are full of other people; regardless of the yellow-stickered daze many may be in while trundling the aisles, good manners are still required and at a premium.

For those who would like to put reduced anxiety in their basket, if you can, the best advice is to shop between 8 a.m. and 10 a.m. on a Monday morning, if shopping in a big city. For those outside of a metropolis, evenings are usually the quietest.

Regardless of what time you embark on your shopping experience, know that most British supermarkets have an unwritten flow. You should start your shop in the aisles nearest to the entrance, which is often where the fresh produce is. An oddity, as surely fresh produce should stay on the refrigerated shelves the

longest so should be found at the 'end' of the supermarket journey, to ensure they spend as little time as possible in your trolley?

It happens to us all, but know that you will face the silent, passive-
aggressive wrath of Brits if you turn your trolley around and go
against the natural flow of shoppers, especially during busy times.
Far better to return to the start of the supermarket and begin
again than perform an inconvenient U-turn.

Block any aisles while scrolling social media on your phone at your
peril. I am always tempted to push my trolley into these people to
see what happens, but thankfully, the deeper, darker fantasies in
my head are yet to become a reality. But be warned.

All shop staff you pass should be acknowledged. Ideally with a
verbal greeting, but at the very least make eye contact and give a
half-smile. No need for a Cheshire-cat grin, just some recognition
that they are a human being, too. When you need to ask them
to where they've moved the sumac, they are much more likely to
want to help you than if you have blanked them as if they are
beneath you the whole time. Incidentally, supermarket workers
will think you are a moron and need medical care if you ask them
'Hello, do you work here?' when they are wearing a fleece in the
brand colours, a headset and name badge.

Some shoppers, especially the chattering middle classes, think the
centre of a narrow aisle is the perfect place to strike up a conversation and catch up with a friend or neighbour they haven't seen for a
bit. A pair of trollies parked two abreast make it next to impossible
for anyone to successfully traverse that aisle. There are two options
available if you do bump into someone and wish to chat with them.
Firstly, arrange to meet in the coffee shop in ten minutes after your
shopping has been completed and loaded into the car. Second, fork
out and buy the supermarket in question and turn it into your own

private shop where there are no other customers to worry about except you and your chum. You're halfway there already.

It is in no way acceptable to eat the food you have selected before you have paid for it. Crumbs from the white baton loaf you've been feeding yourself or your child will fall on the floor, attract vermin, look unsightly, and give the impression you think you are in some way above the rules. You are not. Eat before you arrive at the supermarket, not while walking around inside it.

Britain is leading the way with the concept of reusable bags – well done us. It is good manners (and now really your only option) to arrive with some bags-for-life in your clutches. While most supermarkets do allow you to buy new ones for a small charge, it is good practice to retrain yourself to be compassionate to the environment, and try to reuse bags where possible. Most supermarkets will also let you trade old, tatty ones with holes in for new ones, at no cost. So there's no excuse.

When you have dumped your load onto the supermarket belt, know that if you do not place a 'next customer please' divider at the end of your wares, the shopper behind you will be imagining your slow and painful death as they themselves have to reach for the divider as you were so inconsiderate not to.

A more recent innovation in British supermarkets is the dawn of the self-service checkout. When my local supermarket installed its first staff-free offering, I was greatly amused to hear one of the customers next to me thank the disembodied voice – as it, too, thanked them for shopping. But while I'm not going to stop anyone from showing gratitude to a computer if they want to, I draw the line at public rage. There's no point audibly being frustrated and going all Basil Fawlty at his red Austin 1100. It's only a computer, and you chose to go down that lane rather than wait an extra thirty seconds for a cashier.

Restaurant behaviour

At the start of the twentieth century, restaurants were treated with some social suspicion, especially by the British upper classes, who preferred to eat in their own gilded dining rooms or those of their equally gilded friends. It took the Swiss César Ritz and French Auguste Escoffier to get their stuffier British contemporaries to start enjoying eating out. (Their ventures were also helped by the sudden scarcity of male household staff, thanks to the Boer and the First World wars.) Through their hotels – The Savoy, The Carlton, and latterly the eponymous The Ritz – the master hotelier and master chef made the restaurant concept fashionable, mainly by appealing to women. They knew that if the women wanted to dine in their restaurants, their brow-beaten husbands, who carried the money, would be powerless to resist.

From when they opened their hotel on Piccadilly in 1905, there is a wonderful story of Ritz and Escoffier sitting in the restaurant, testing out numerous shades of pink lampshade to find the most complimentary colour. They wanted to make the lighting in their grand restaurant so flattering for their female patrons that they would all demand to return again and again. Ritz also came up with the idea of screwing in little brass hooks under the arms of half of the chairs on which ladies could hook their bags, rather than put them on the floor or have them in their laps. Some of these hooks remain on the chairs in the hotel today – as do the pink lampshades.*

---

* The Ritz has another special place in British dining history. It was the first restaurant where Queen Elizabeth, the Queen Mother, ordered from a menu for the very first time. (Previously she would have just asked the nearby chef to make her whatever she fancied.)

As a nation, many of us are now fortunate enough to be able to dine out, whether it's in the marble-columned dining room of The Ritz or at a sticky table in the local greasy spoon. The degrees of etiquette displayed vary between both those ends of the culinary spectrum – but the guiding principles of hospitality and dining with others are universal.

With most restaurants now belonging to a chain or a restaurant group, and a rise in an appreciation of international flavours, quirky individual British restaurants are few and far between. Whatever the cuisine, one way for a restaurant to annoy a British diner is to invoke the American standard of clearing empty dishes while there are other diners at the table still eating. While well-intentioned, this purgation of plates goes against one of the key tenets of eating: that it is a tasty communal experience, to be enjoyed more or less at the same time as everyone else. Having one diner sit there, devoid of dinnerware, staring at those still munching is distinctly unappetising.

Arrival procedure and seating

If one party has invited another out for dinner, the host is the one who should arrive first. If the reservation is for eight o'clock, the host should arrive at ten to eight to check that everything is in order and that there are no unexpected surprises. This extra ten minutes is essential, not just for alerting the welcome staff to your imminent arrival but also for saving face if something has gone wrong. A host's face will turn as red as lobster bisque if they are told they made the reservation for the wrong day while they stand next to their dining companions.

In an ideal world, a restaurant would have a decent-sized waiting area for people to loiter in while the rest of the party gathers. But the greedy thinking from proprietors today is why make guests feel comfortable when you can have no holding area and instead

193

squeeze in three more tables on the restaurant floor? Future diners are packed in at the front like the cannelloni de carne they're about to order.

It is, therefore, understandable if hosts wish to wait for their guests at the table, in the interest of not creating a health-and-safety incident at the front door. If you are there a few minutes before your guests, be sure to check with the restaurant that your allotted time will only begin at the official start of your reservation and not when you sit down.

Once seated and waiting, it is fine to nibble on the naan or swallow some sourdough, but it is not good manners to purloin any other food or drink (except water) until the entire party has gathered. In those few moments of calm limbo when a host is waiting for their guests, they can also take a moment to work out where best to seat them. Seating plans are not just for private houses. The best seats always go to the guests. As for which these are, it depends on the restaurant. If you've taken them up the Shard, for example, the best seats will be facing the view of London, with their backs to the restaurant. But for establishments at lower altitudes, often it is the reverse, with guests facing into the restaurant and not having to stare at walls.

Restaurants now have militant attitudes towards how long each party can stay for, not only telling you upon booking (which is fair enough) but then curtly citing the time they need the table back when you arrive (awful). Not really the mark of gracious hospitality, especially when you are the ones paying for it. Thus, once everyone is assembled, ordering should begin.

Ordering food

The requirements for this have changed, and now each guest is expected to order for themselves. In a bygone age, the host would gather everyone's choices and then relay them to the waiter. A lovely idea, but totally impractical today, when most cannot begin to entertain ordering something without modifying it to their exact taste. The new rule is, if you must, you can make one modification (no tomato, for example). But if your burger has become a salad by the time you've finished ordering it, then something's gone wrong.

Each member of the waiting staff you encounter will ask you whether you have any allergies. I was recently asked it six times in the space of ten minutes, which was quite a feat. The new custom is to remain silent to allow those who may have something to say to speak, but if, after a silent pause, no one says anything, you may confidently deflect the waiter's inquisition as to your consociation's nutritional vulnerabilities.

If you are being entertained in a restaurant and you know you are not paying, do not automatically pick the most expensive item from the menu – opt instead for something of a mid- to lower price point. There are two exceptions. Firstly, if your host announces they are having the Dover sole (or whatever the priciest product is). Or if your host is a multimillionaire. Although it would still be a touch vulgar to take such blatant advantage of their wealth.

Regardless of the fiscal arrangements of your table, everyone wants to order the same number of courses and drinks, rather than one person being overly abstemious or gluttonous. It makes for a much better end to the evening and splitting the bill by the number of diners is easier. If a friend starts getting out their phone's calculator to work out the sum total of what they had, it is best to make a mental note not to invite them to such events in the future, as they clearly are overly worried about their finances so are best left at home.

If one person did have a significantly lavish, pricier dish, or drank alcohol when no one else did, however, they should insist on paying an extra ten pounds, for example, and then the rest of the bill is still divided by the number of diners.

Any calculations should be done swiftly and without too much fuss. Remember, Brits don't love public displays of finance, and nothing ruins a nice meal with friends more than maths.

Ordering wine

Wine is, conventionally, paired with food, but for some time now the thinking has been that it is better paired with people. Fish may go the best with a crisp white wine, but if Great-Aunt Maud loves a bold claret, she is probably going to want that regardless of what meat is in front of her.

This switch has given rise to sommeliers arriving before the food has been chosen to take a drinks order. I would argue this is better done the other way round, with the food selected first and the drinks ordered last. There is no issue if you politely ask the sommelier to return in a few minutes.

Nor should hosts with a more rudimentary knowledge of wine be afraid to ask the sommelier's assistance in picking something out for the table, whether that's to pair with the menu or your budget. You can gesture at the price point you are thinking, without anyone except you and the wine help seeing, and say, 'Perhaps something like this?' They will get the message and suggest a bottle around a similar cost.

When the bottle arrives, it is presented to the host or whoever ordered it, so they can check the label. This is a piece of French-style theatre, mainly, but it's amazing how many people don't check and end up with the wrong year or totally wrong wine altogether.

A small serving of the wine is poured into a glass for the host to check. The main objective here is to see if it is corked, not if you don't like it. If it is corked, you will know very quickly as it will stink of gone-off mushrooms. If the full-bodied pinot you've just pressed to your lips is oakier than you'd really want, you are welcome to reject the bottle, but as they have just opened it for you, you'll be paying for it and the new selection. You'll become their ideal customer. When testing, remember you are not at a wine-tasting event, so the manner in which you taste must be different. Swirling the glass around dramatically and giving such a pronounced sniff they can hear it in the private dining room is not correct in any way. And definitely don't swirl it around in your mouth before spitting it out. Swallow!

Getting a waiter's attention

Waiters are called over to the table by non-verbal communication alone. There should be no noise, either by calling out 'waiter?' (those who think using the French *garçon* adds charm are dramatically misguided) or by clicking your fingers. Keep your hand at the level of your eye and lean back slightly, drawing yourself away from the epicentre of the table, and that should work on well-trained staff.

Sharing food

While this was totally verboten when the last round of etiquette books was written, dining has changed. The influx of different cuisines from around the world, many of which have a less structured approach than traditional British or French dining, has meant we often share little bits of bigger dishes with our company, or multiple smaller dishes, rather than just order one thing for ourselves.

But the usual British rule of putting others before ourselves still applies, whatever the food's country of origin. All dishes must be offered to each side of us before we help ourselves. Hopefully spoons or serving equipment are provided by the restaurant and we are not expected to use the same cutlery we're about to stick in our mouths to serve. Ask for new cutlery in such an upsetting instance.

The now familiar 'Sarah, would you like any baba ganoush?' tactic (see page 83) can be used to get dishes passed to you that you cannot easily reach, if other diners haven't clocked you are in desperate need of some aubergine.

When dining in the more traditional style of a dish per person, it is best not to offer chunks of your food to your loved one on your fork, passing it across the table as the sauce drips off and makes a mischief of the tablecloth. Instead, ask for a small bread plate, place the food on the plate, and pass the plate. Much more elegant.

Should there just be one chunk of whatever dish left, British good manners means we have to put ourselves last and offer it all around the table, in the vain hope that no one else wants it. If someone doesn't announce they'll have the last floret of cauliflower cheese, you're in luck and can help yourself. If they do, however, it's a crying shame, but at least you still have your good manners.

Paying the bill

The non-verbal signal we developed to let a waiter know, from some distance, that you require the bill is to sign a cheque in mid-air. In the days of chip-and-pin and contactless payments, you could argue this is now redundant. Perhaps using your index finger to punch your four-digit code into thin air is more appropriate? Maybe. But it's also ridiculous. The squiggle remains universally and globally known.

If I were prime minister, I would allow all patrons to be able to leave the table without paying after ten minutes of sitting with the bill in front of them but no card machine brought. Sadly, however, I am not yet in high office, and this practice remains illegal.

There is hope, however, with some restaurants having discreet QR codes in the middle of the table. Once scanned, the bill is displayed, and payment can be made using the phone's built-in wallet or entering card details. Most of these gizmos allow bills to be split, too. Unless you are a Luddite of the highest order, this is much easier for everyone involved and a good use of modern technology for a more mannerly exit.

Tipping

Britain does not have the tipping culture that many other countries do. This is generally a good thing, if you ask me, although one cannot fault the efficiency of the service industry in the United States.

American staff may sometimes be a bit brash in their approach ('Hello, my name is Kandi and I'll be the server guiding your experience today'), but as they are all so badly paid, they have to rely on getting a decent gratuity to keep the wolf from the door. In Britain, tips and service charges are often pooled and split equally amongst the entire team. That may be more in keeping with our nation's democratic sensibilities, but can lead to a handful of staff carrying the rest of their colleagues.

Tourists in the UK should note that most restaurants, especially chains, will have automatically added an 'optional service charge' to the bottom of the bill. This is now 13.5 per cent in most restaurants, having very recently risen from 12.5 per cent. The word 'optional' is beguiling, as most Brits wouldn't dare be so bold as to ask for that to be removed, especially as we'd have to flag this to the server we're about to short-change. But, in theory, it can be wiped from the bill, either as you wish to leave a cash tip (in which case 10 per cent is fine – the extra 2.5–3.5 per cent is to cover the card processing fee) or because you are so enraged about the service that you wish to make a point. Remember that if there is an issue with a dish, you should ask for the cost of it to be removed from the bill; withholding a service charge is not the way to make a point about what you ate.

The most considerate diners will ask their waiter if they get the tip directly. A simple and firm 'yes' is what you are looking for; anything else means they are being too loyal and trying to avoid telling you they don't. Leaving cash, in this instance, is the way forward.

Doggie bags

It will come as no surprise to many people that the practice of taking home leftover food from over-piled plates comes from America. Doggie bags are so-called as we go through the charade that these morsels will be fed to the waiting pooch at home, all the while knowing full well that the dog's not getting any of it. Indeed, in some instances, there isn't even a dog.

While these bags became a thing in America during the Second World War to avoid waste (first documented in San Francisco in 1943), the concept of taking food home from a meal is much older. From ancient times up until the start of the eighteenth century, it was not unusual for guests to bring their own cutlery and napkins to dine, and taking home leftover food was not seen as offensive – as the service à la russe style of dining we know today (set course after set course) was not present. Instead, food was laid out à la française in the middle of the table, almost like what we'd now call a buffet.

But, in the age of such excessive food waste and food poverty, any Anglo aversion to waddling down Piccadilly with some shunned lemon jumbles following a hefty tea has all but gone. A modification to the manners of doggie bags (now more often boxes) would be to only accept one if the restaurant offers, or ask if you see others with them.

Behind closed doors: Private members' clubs

Emerging from the old coffee houses of the seventeenth century, Britain – and London in particular – is awash with private members' clubs, especially compared to other countries where the concept of exclusive societies behind closed doors just would not work. While in the 1800s there were around 400 of these institutions, their numbers now are much lower, with just over sixty still functioning – some clinging to the wreckage, trying to avoid being washed away by changing attitudes and financial burdens.

To many, these buildings are the zenith of British society, full of manners and codes of behaviour, and the club ingénue should first be aware that while there are some common threads, each club has different rules. It would be impossible to know all the rules for every club, and if you are being hosted in a club by your friend or business contact, it is easiest to ask them in advance what the general procedure is and what you are expected to wear. No one is meant to know everything, but navigating Club Land's eccentricities is not where you want to risk it and take an educated guess.

While freedom of choice and expression may be sweeping the rest of the nation, it has yet to penetrate some of these older and more hallowed halls. At the time of writing, fourteen of the London clubs do not allow female members – although certain patrons of the more traditional clubs are at pains to point out that there are clubs that only allow women and not men. Two clubs don't even allow female visitors to cross the threshold, so concerned are they about their male members. It's often hard to work out if they're running a private members' club or a dark room in Soho.

Generally, the idea of any club is that it is a home away from home. Thus, a lot of the rules of a private house apply. These clubs are not meant to be secret, however, but merely safe havens in order for their members to talk freely and openly about whatever their interests are. And each club, historically, has a raison d'être to distinguish it from other clubs. For example, the Garrick Club is home to those in the arts and theatre, the Carlton Club is a collection of people who identify as Conservative, the Caledonian Club houses people who know their way around a haggis, whereas the common thread for Pratt's club remains an enigma.

Before leaving your own house to go to one of these clubs, you must enquire about the dress code. This will vary from club to club and even between rooms within each club. For example, some will have areas where men must wear a tie; others will have cordoned-off sections where the idea of an open neck will not scandalise anyone. Club websites often list their requirements, but hosts need to be crystal-clear to their guests as to what is expected of them. Some clubs may have spare ties to lend out, but having to redress in reception is never a good look. Other more liberal clubs may erroneously boast that, as an antidote to the stuffier clubs, they do not have a dress code, and anyone can wear whatever they like . . . except a suit and tie. Which, in itself, is a dress code. But would they be a British institution without a dress code?

Once inside, be on the lookout for any particular traditions of that club. For example, Brooks's on St James's, where you are presented with a silver tankard of Champagne once you are seated in the bar. A thoughtful host will flag these quirks before they happen, so virgin guests are not alarmed.

One rule that is consistent for all clubs, including the more relaxed, contemporary ones such as Soho House, is the absolute veto on photography. (Yes, I know we have all probably seen photos of opaque drinks with red chilis in them posted on social media, but it's against the rules and smacks of showing off, which we don't tend to like in Britain.) This photographic ban is to protect the privacy of other members, who may or may not be people of note; but – frankly – in an age where apparently everything has to be a photo moment and documented, it's quite refreshing to know you are not going to have to pose and grin for a photo no one is ever going to look at again once it's been shared to Facebook. The exception to this rule would be private event spaces within the clubs – maybe hired for a birthday dinner or similar. There, photos may be taken unless told otherwise.

Should you enjoy your visit to your friend's club, you may wish to consider becoming a member. But get the term right – you do not 'apply', you are 'proposed'. The manners surrounding the membership of these institutions are nearly as complicated as knowing which dress code applies when and in which room. In true British style, there is even a hierarchy between the types of members: those who are full members of the club rank higher than those who are visiting as part of a reciprocal arrangement with another club.

You often have to have two people propose you, and usually they will each need to write a letter of proposition, which serves as a character reference. Many clubs have very long waiting lists, so don't expect a quick answer unless you are some great luminary. In effect, the vetting procedure is to see if the person being proposed is a 'good chap', and the person doing the proposing is often scrutinised as much as the person they are advocating for. If an application is rejected, it often speaks more about the person proposing than the blackballed bod. (Often, no further clarity or reasoning is given by the club for the rejection.)

Finally, if you are visiting a club, just like when you go to someone's house, it is at the expense of the host, and they are solely responsible for the bill. Keep that in mind when ordering but, just like with a restaurant, if they announce they are having the Kobe beef you can follow suit and pick whatever you like on the menu. The menu guests get given by staff may not have the prices listed, but a rudimentary knowledge of food will help you work out which the more expensive dishes are. You are, however, expected to reciprocate the hospitality another time in the not-too-distant future, unless you wish to kill the connection. Invite them to your house, a restaurant or host them at the club yourself – should you be accepted.

Pubiquette

The pub (a contraction of 'public house') is a distinctly British institution that is not seen anywhere else overseas. Pubs come in all shapes and sizes: some are only drinking pubs, some serve food, while others serve such good-quality food, presented in stacks and towers with jus and reductions coming out of every artichoke, that they are often mistaken for a restaurant.

Also in existence in Britain are sports pubs. These are ones where sizeable plasma screens are wall-mounted around the place at some height, ready for people to stand nearby and make noises no one really understands, while the gathered throng stares up at large expanses of green. For those who do not like sports and feel intimidated by the presence of a television showing Sky Sports, these are not the places for you.

Aside from the (relatively) cheaper cost of alcohol, one of the reasons that pubs hold such a special place in the hearts of many Brits is the fact they allow dogs. You'll often find small china bowls positioned strategically around the floor of the pub, in order for canines to quench their thirst while their owners are doing the same at a marginally higher altitude. (For absolute clarity for pub newbies, the liquid in the dog bowls is water and nothing else.)

My pub-loving friend Jonathan was once on holiday for the first time in Florida, and on exploring his host's neighbourhood one evening, spotted a retired couple sitting in their garage, with the garage door open, drinks in hand. Jonathan asked what they were doing, only to be told by his friend that they, along with many others of a similar age, did that almost every night in the hope of finding someone to talk to. If America had a pub culture, those poor Floridian fossils wouldn't have had to resort to driveway drinking.

A key rule of the British pub is that you are never alone. You can walk into a pub solo and – so long as you don't look or act like a total weirdo – always find someone to talk to without too much effort. If it's not any of the other patrons, the staff will chat with you from behind the bar as they pump out whatever you've requested. In a British pub, standing by yourself at a bar is not always a sign of a reclusive alcoholic. Other patrons may be on their own, too, and even if they have brought friends, they are usually up for meeting new people and engaging in some enjoyable jaw action. No one will ever be lonely in a pub. This rule is especially true for drinking pubs, as opposed to gastropubs, where people have arrived with friends and family to enjoy the food and delicious conversation with their own party.

The usual rules for meeting new people, however, do not apply. The arm outstretched, broad smile and 'how do you do' stuff from the beginning of this book is all to be totally forgotten when ensconced in a pub. Instead, use dry British humour or make a passing observation about the day's weather to begin your chat.

Although not always the case today, if a group of friends are going to the pub, it is thought to be good manners for each friend to take it in turns to 'get a round in'. This means a round of drinks. For example, Freddie buys for him and the five others assembled at the start. Then Anna goes next and buys drinks for everyone when the cups have run dry. And so on. This, however, can be pretty irresponsible, and doesn't really work or balance out if you are only going for one or two. It is also, dare I say it, a bit blokey. For those not having the same yeasty concoction, you do not need to participate in the round – or you may choose to do a micro-round. A group of girlfriends may split the price of a bottle of wine, for example.

But some say that this tradition of rounds is as sacred as the changing of the guard at Buckingham Palace and Garter Day at Windsor. In the north of England, where they are arguably more up for heavier drinking than their south-eastern counterparts, this is probably very much still done – especially on the weekend. But, wherever you are, if you are not up for excessive drinking to the power of the number of people in your party, then it is fine to announce 'I'm on my own' upon arrival.

If you are all going in for rounds, and that has been agreed, there is, however, a widely held belief that one of the worst things you can do in a pub is duck out of paying for a round of drinks for friends. Jordan North, my close personal friend, has spent far too much of his time worrying about this. He has very strong feelings about this social crime and vehemently calls round-dodgers 'the worst sort of people'. He even suggests that there should be some sort of searchable national database for those who repeatedly dodge rounds.

Some – often Americans – believe that throwing down some cash on the table when they want to leave will be met with gracious thanks. You may as well slap everyone in the face if you do that. It is not the same as paying for a round.

When it comes to ordering in a pub, do not expect table service. You're not on the Continent. You have to go to them. There are some pubs where this happens, but they are few and far between. During the summer months in the larger cities and chocolate-box villages, Brits are often amused to see groups of tourists politely sitting at a table outside, waiting to be served. The correct way to order is to mince on up to the bar and look as friendly as possible. Frankly, those who have come alone may be blocking you actually getting to the bar and drawing the attention of the staff, so you might need to awkwardly muscle your way in while apologising out loud or wearing a plaintive expression. Be sure to clock if there is already a gaggle of people waiting, as queue jumping is another of the big British sins. Pub queues tend to be horizontal to the bar, and any barperson worth their salt should remember the order in which everyone arrived.

Eye contact and non-verbal communication are the keys to getting a barperson's attention. An upward nod from the chin also helps once you have locked irises. I once put my hand up in the air and was quickly reminded I wasn't at school.

It is good to know exactly what you are ordering the moment you get their attention, or else they are likely to move on to the next patron, especially during busy periods. Wasted time is money. Use your mobile to note down what each person wants rather than try to remember or call back to your posse and have them shout their order across the room.

Unless you are illiterate or blind, do not ask the publican what beers they have on tap if you are standing in full view of the beer pumps on the bar, labels facing out. They are likely to take you for a fool or think you are taking the proverbial.

Tipping is not customary in pubs. In cocktail bars, where they have spent minutes faffing over your drink and sticking an umbrella in it, it is more customary to slip them a little something, but in a pub, all you need to do is round up and tell them to keep the change, if at all.

Cancelling plans

Cancel culture is upon us, and not just in the sense that people are now sent into exile if they say something without engaging their brain or having a rational thought first. The biggest form of cancel culture, and one that will linger for longer, is that of friends cancelling last minute – or 'bailing', as the youth would say (I am told I am no longer one of them).

A friend clears their diary to see their chum, and turns down other invitations (sometimes better ones) only for the social rug to be whipped out from beneath them at the last minute. The friend 'isn't feeling too well'. If the slighted one is really unlucky, they'll turn to Instagram a few hours later to see the (thick, frankly) friend posting about moving and grooving with others instead of poor old Billy No Mates. (If that does happen, you have every right to never talk to that friend again, or give them an earful when and if you next communicate.)

Bailing is particularly rife in the bigger, faster-paced cities. Perhaps this is down to inhabitants making plans weeks and weeks in advance. By the time the appointed date comes round, life has got in the way and how they feel now about going out after work for drinks is different from how it felt two months ago when they committed.

As with anything, there are manners around cancelling plans. First off, don't look at it as a cancellation, look at it as a postponement. You should really only cancel on inanimate things like gym memberships and niche streaming services. Humans have feelings, treadmills don't. There are also better times to bail and worse times. Cancelling with a decent notice period is preferable, ideally weeks and weeks, but is it a bail if more than forty-eight hours is given?

As already noted, when declining invitations, there is no need to give a specific reason. But when cancelling at the eleventh hour, a specific (and hopefully honest) reason needs to be provided pretty damn quickly. The whole thing must be done by a telephone call and not a lazy text. Genuine regret must be offered, and any costs incurred – such as a deposit or charge for a restaurant reservation – must be paid in full by the one cancelling.

It is the politer route to offer a choice of your next available dates as to when you can see them. Although not guaranteed, this can take the sting out of the supposed rejection, especially for the more anxious millennials and Gen Zers. Once a new date has been set, it is best to add a notation to your calendar entry such as 'Do not cancel', to ensure you don't become a repeat offender. Should the other party cancel, of course, you have no right to be annoyed in any way and must totally understand, even if you are furious with them.

Remember that all these attendance U-turns frustrate abandoned hosts and solitary friends up and down the land, and invalidate any genuine reason to pull out of something as and when tragic life moments happen. You should only really cancel if you have to.

Complaining

Brits are not known to be great complainers, mainly due to our aversion to confrontation. We usually remain tight-lipped in the face of terrible service, or become boorish and overbearing. Neither option is the way forward. Yet we don't want to become like our American cousins, who are highly trained in the art of the complaint (probably as they have a much more cut-throat service culture than we do; one cold quesadilla and you're out).

Nothing summarises that first British approach than a scene in *Fawlty Towers* where two older ladies are ferociously complaining to each other about how awful it all is. When Basil Fawlty, the manager, looms over them to check if everything is okay, they both break into broad beaming smiles and reassure him it's all perfect.

Remember that good establishments will want to offer a fair and decent experience to their patrons and should be open to feedback. If they are not, then they are perhaps better-suited to jobs that do not involve the Great British Public.

The way to complain effectively is to first strip all emotion from the complaint, which you would think most Brits would be good at doing, coming from one of the world's less emotional nations. All complaints should be factual. 'This happened, and then this happened, but we expected something else.' You then leave the ball in the court of the waiter or manager to offer a resolution.

It is important to remember that to ensure you do not lose your consumer rights, you complain at the time of the issue and do not wait days and weeks before you say something. Should it get all nasty and blow up, the law will not be on your side if you have not given the business a chance to deal with your issue directly and in a timely manner. There is also an argument for hosts stepping away from the table to deal with any issues rather than turning the protest into a show trial, playing to the gallery that is your assembled company. Waiting staff and restaurateurs do not need to be fed to the lions while you preside over the mini-coliseum that is your table.

If you are not satisfied with the resolution given on the day, a crisp letter or stern email can be sent the next day. That'll show 'em. You can also leave an online review on a reputable review site, but posting on your Instagram story is tedious and as effective as an ejector seat in a helicopter.

It is, however, good to get into the habit of leaving as many positive reviews as you do negative ones. Very few people realise that you can click on the reviewer's name and see all the other recent reviews they have posted, which gives people a rough idea as to how seriously to take the complaint.

Spotting people of note

This is a topic that has been absent from manners books until now, perhaps due to the fact that we now have more 'celebrities' and people of public interest than ever before. In London and the bigger British cities, they say you are never more than six feet away from an influencer. Time to break some new etiquette ground.

It would be very churlish for the famous to be dismissive to someone who came up to say hello – most of those people are generally only notable thanks to a sizeable public following. But fans should pause to establish the context of where they have found their idol. If they are clearly working – standing on a street corner with a camera crew around them, for example – then it is fair enough to want to acknowledge them. If the celebrity is clearly enjoying themselves in a non-work capacity, perhaps at a restaurant table with friends, then it is best not to say anything, if you can help it. Should you happen to see them in the lavatories or when leaving the restaurant, it's okay to say a very quick hello, but be very hesitant to ask for a photograph.

There is, also, an etiquette for those who get spotted. The best example of perfect manners in such a scenario is Claudia Winkleman, the beloved television presenter, who tells of having frequently been stopped in the street by excited fans, who after several moments then ask 'Please may I have your autograph, Davina?' – having mistaken her for another brunette female TV host. (Claudia does not burst their bubble, but instead signs 'With lots of love, Davina McCall' and walks on.)

CHAPTER EIGHT

No Brown in Town

In Britain, there used to be an old adage that it was the height of bad manners to be overdressed. It showed the person had gone to too much effort, which was thus pronounced vulgar. Frankly, that is an overstated and outdated belief. If only more people were overdressed today! It's not a concern many now have.

What we wear is an extension of ourselves, an expression of our personality and how we see those who are attending or hosting an event. By making an effort, we pay the greatest compliment to the host and their guests – aside from clearing time in one's hectic social calendar and turning up in the first place.

Although to some modern minds, having anyone give them a set of rules they are expected to follow on how to dress can be an insult and restriction to their liberty, once they get over themselves, they generally do see that a dress code can be a great leveller. When people are dressed in the same or similar clothing, it helps with conversation and everyone's ability to mix. Where they are dressed differently, things can get tricky.

A few years ago, while I was in Dubai for work, my friend invited me to be her guest at a party at a private members' club. The dress code was black tie, she told me. Black tie! For Dubai, this was super formal and almost unheard of, but I'm never one to turn my nose up at the chance to wear black tie, so I gladly accepted. What hadn't been mentioned was that there was a *second* dress code on the invitation.

I arrived at the club on a warm but comfortable evening, my patent leather shoes doing a decent job reflecting the bright lights of the phallic Burj Khalifa looming above us. But I started to panic as I clocked guest after guest alighting from their cars in 1970s fancy dress. One could hardly move without seeing rose-tinted glasses, comedy wigs and flapping flares. My midnight-blue and white ensemble was somewhat of a stark contrast. Once inside, my horror was compounded as the venue's décor continued the seventies theme. I stood out like a sore thumb, and now I certainly did not feel like partying. There were only two other men dressed in black tie – the 150 or so others all looked like they were attending a Rolling Stones fan convention.

Prior to that incident, I had prided myself on being able to make conversation with anyone of sound mind and from any walk of life. To say I struggled that evening is an understatement. No one in fancy dress wanted to talk to me. I could see their micro- and macro-expressions of disdain as I approached, trying to make my body language as open and inviting as possible. It wasn't enough. I simply looked too different from them, and so, purely based on my appearance, they were writing me off as a threat. And probably a 'snob', as well, seeing as I was bedecked in a dress code that, to many, has certain class connotations.

Guess who I spent the evening talking to? Yes – the two other men in black tie. They, too, admitted they didn't feel very comfortable.

The blaring music, which made everyone's uvulas retreat, didn't help fuel the conversation, either. I left after ninety protracted and painful minutes. I couldn't take it any longer and decided to write this one off.

Whose fault was it? Was it my friend's for not flagging both dress codes? Was it mine for not asking to see the invitation itself? (Which, it turns out, was designed in a retro-1970s fashion.) Or was it the hosts', for picking two such disparate dress codes? We're all to blame, really. Had we been dressed the same, it would have dramatically changed my experience of that night.

One of the highlights of the British social season is the Glyndebourne Festival Opera, which since 1934 has been held each summer at an old manor house in Sussex. The dress code is black tie and has been since the festival's debut. As Jo Bryant, my friend and colleague at The English Manner, always tells our classes, it was explained by Glyndebourne, until recently, that dressing up was not meant to be a way to inconvenience guests but a sign of respect to the performers. The evening dress code added a sense of occasion and put the attendees in the mindset that they were about to enjoy a world-class performance. If that dress code was not in place, what would be the difference between sitting at home in comfortable clothes, listening to a pre-recorded track, and actually getting to live and be in the moment, sharing an experience never to be exactly repeated?

Ahead of our Easter school holidays, when we would all (of course) be locked away, diligently revising for the looming exams and not making films recreating the Bible with Beanie Babies, the headmaster at school, Dr Stephen Spurr, would encourage us to revise in our school uniform. He stressed that if we tried to revise in what is now called 'loungewear', we would find it very hard to get into the right mental headspace to learn. He had a valid point.

I would find it impossible to do my job if I turned up to teach etiquette while wearing my gym clothes. I am indeed writing this very section of this book in full morning dress.

But if you have a dress code, it must help and not hinder. The current British uneasiness with enforcing dress codes has led to ambiguous words and twisted phraseology such as 'smart', 'formal' and (as I saw once) 'lounge suits with a hint of inner child'. What the Dickens does all that mean? One person's smart is another's casual. Formal to one is a suit, to another it's white tie and tails. If guests are left having to make too many enquiries as to what they are expected to wear, their host has failed them before the first cork's even been popped. Having a set of rules and parameters is helpful, and helps narrow down what could be endless choices and options of clothes for guests to wear.

In Britain, there are a few more dress codes to worry about than in other countries, which can trip up those new to the concept. Look up the whole Trump family during the 2019 state banquet at Buckingham Palace if you want to see a whole rack of interesting interpretations of white tie.

Our class system, too, informs people's choices and our opinions on what they should wear. You only have to compare the always present, pick-apart coverage of red-carpet events in the UK and US to see the differing opinions of the two countries. In the United States, outlets like *E!* will do articles on best and worst dressed, what the colour stitching on each dress means, and whether a chunky bangle on the wrist of a popstar gives us all a clue as to the name of their new album. Cut to the MailOnline in Britain, and we have similar articles – but they tend to focus more on whether a person's outfit was *appropriate* for the event. Someone in a dress with cut-out sections in California would not raise any eyebrows in the US, but there would be a public cry of outrage should a Brit turn up in a similar garment to the BAFTAs. Should the wrong material be worn for the wrong time of day, then woe betide the sartorial criminal the next morning.

Looking back at the press coverage Meghan, the Duchess of Sussex, got while she was a working member of the Royal Family, there were many articles on her 'fashion faux pas'. I am not a stylist by any means, but reviewing these articles, which were relentless, the sins were mainly because of the context of the occasion, rather than critiquing whether a dress was on trend or if it fitted the duchess. When the engagement of Prince Harry and Meghan was announced in 2017, the B-side of the British coverage was her lack of tights as they posed and pouted around the sunken garden at Kensington Palace. While there is no codified protocol rule on tights for members of the Royal Family, it is generally believed that Queen Elizabeth, like many of her generation, preferred ladies to wear tights with skirts and dresses, believing that a good-quality piece of silk could help 'finish' the leg and outfit.

Although examples are not in the hundreds of thousands, some of our restaurants, especially in London, have dress codes, as singer Jess Glynne found out a few years ago. Back in July 2020, Ms Glynne decided she was above the clearly stated dress code on the restaurant Sexy Fish's website. Which, for those not familiar with it, is: 'We kindly ask all guests DO NOT wear any sportswear, loungewear, and beachwear including tracksuits, gym leggings, shorts, flip flops, beach sliders and caps. Gentlemen are permitted to wear smart shorts and open-toed sandals, however not after 7pm.'

Ms Glynne arrived at the Asian-inspired restaurant in a hoodie, leggings and peaked cap. She might be able to read music, but obviously fell short of reading websites. She was violating several of their sartorial policies, and then, rather than engaging in a reasoned debate with the staff like an adult, she churlishly took to social media to vent. It didn't go in her favour, as most Brits resented the fact that she apparently thought her purported star power would override the restaurant's policy.

Approaching this topic with one foot firmly in the here and now, where so much of what people wear (especially in bigger cities) is much less rigidly gender-specific, I should make it clear that while there is a form for 'men' and 'women', anyone can wear whichever form they like, so long as they follow the suggested parameters for the traditionally masculine or feminine form. If a woman wants to wear a dinner jacket ensemble, then so be it. If a male-presenting person wants to wear a ballgown to a dance, then they can knock themselves out; they'll probably look great and not upset the etiquette police if they follow the standard guidelines. While clothes do not have a gender, what follows will largely refer to the 'conventional' masculine and feminine forms; however, people are open to follow whichever they please.

But, whatever we wear, the manners around dress codes are not to be confused with style. You are not about to read advice from me on colour-blocking, body shape and whether a pearl necklace looks best on a longer or shorter neck. All the following etiquette suggestions on clothes and their context are merely to give you a strong steer in the right direction when you have to follow a stated dress code. (Do I even need to say that deliberately ignoring a dress code for a party is really bad form? If you don't like the dress code, just don't accept the invitation.)

Top hat and tails: White tie

Seen on invitations as 'white tie' or 'full evening dress', this is the grandest and most elegant dress code in Britain, although it is rarely seen outside of royal environs. Even then, it makes a few dazzling appearances a year, namely at state banquets and the annual diplomatic reception. Many may see it in their own homes, but only while sitting on their sofas watching *Downton Abbey* or *The Crown*.

It is incredibly cumbersome and hard to get right, which is perhaps why it has all but vanished from British wardrobes. If it is to be worn, an immaculate appearance is expected – even former prime minister Boris Johnson, not known for his personal grooming, managed to not look too bad in white tie.

Other countries have disposed of the need for this evening dress code for their state dinners: George H. W. Bush retired it from American official usage, before his son, George W. Bush, bought it back as a one-off in 2007 for Queen Elizabeth II, to mark the fifteenth anniversary of Her Majesty's first visit to the US. (Prince Philip reportedly did not like this dress code, so I am not sure how delighted he would have been at America's gesture.)

The male form of this dress, which dates back to the middle of the nineteenth century, features clothes that are either black or white. Colour may only be present if 'decorations' are to be worn (medals and sashes, not Christmas baubles). Silk top hats are correct, but only when enjoying a party outdoors (which in Britain, at night, is not very often). Due to their expense and scarcity (production stopped on them in 1968), no one really bothers with these any more. (Incidentally, top hats are so-called due to their height – not, as some insist, because they were only worn by 'the top people'.)

Moving down the body, we come to the dress shirt. This should be pristine white and heavily starched to within an inch of its life. (Spray starch is not starch, incidentally. Proper starch comes in powder form and requires a bit more skill than pointing and spraying.) The starch will help the winged collar stay erect and not go floppy as the night goes on. The shirt is fastened with white dress studs, often mother-of-pearl or black onyx.

Around the neck should be a white bow tie, which should come as no shock to anyone, given this dress code's name. It is strongly advised to have immaculately clean hands before tying, as white marcella is so unforgiving. While a pretied bow tie may be more frequently seen for the less dressy black tie, attendees at any white tie function should just decline the invitation upon receipt if they are thinking of attending with a ready-made one. Queen Elizabeth II liked to gently boast she could spot a fake one a mile off, although given how cheap and obvious fake ones look, I am not sure this was as much a talent as Her late Majesty thought it was.

The black peaked-lapel tailcoat cuts away at the waist and is never fastened, and should stop in line with the back of the knee joint. When taking your seat, be sure not to sit on the tails. Carefully part them when sitting down. A theatrical flick is only acceptable if you have one of the philharmonics in front of you. Under the tailcoat is the white waistcoat, often low-cut and in a pique honeycomb material. All buttons on these waistcoats are fastened.

The trousers, held up by braces, match the material of the jacket but have two braids of silk running down the outside of each leg. This is such a minor detail and one that really only fastidious Brits would pay attention to, but a fun game to play at events with this dress code. When we filmed the special on-location edition of ITV's *This Morning* at Highclere Castle to promote the *Downton Abbey* film, I was kitted out in white tie from a costumier. The trousers had only one braid running down the leg. You can imagine the scene when I spotted it. (Obviously, in reality, I said nothing – as, like many Brits, I don't like confrontation.)

Shoes should be full-cut patent black leather, set off by some long black silk evening socks. There used to be a rule that people did not wear a watch to evening events – presumably as it was the last event of the day and you had nowhere else to go. Life is very different now, and watches are needed. You may wear one, so long as it's not too chunky and noticeable.

The female form for white tie requires long, sweeping gowns in opulent fabrics that touch the floor. But while the dresses may flow, the hair should not. Those with long hair should wear it neatly tied up. The reasoning behind this was if there was to be dancing (and historically, dancing was more often on the cards than it is today), it would prevent some split ends whipping the face of the woman's dance partner as they did a natural spin turn.

On top of the tidy hair can be a tiara, but not always. Of course, in the United Kingdom, we even have rules for jewels. Only wear a tiara if the occasion calls for it: the invitation will say 'Decorations' next to the dress code. Unless you are a royal princess by birth, you can only wear one if you are married and have one in your family. It's seen as very vulgar to buy a tiara, even if you are made of money. Far smarter to have one handed down the generations to you. But going tiara-less is no sin at all. There are more people today without them at state banquets than with. During the White House dinner for the United Kingdom in 2007, Laura Bush did not wear a tiara. No issues, as there are very few tiaras in Texas.

Royal dress watchers like me have been at first alarmed, and then intrigued, to see members of the Royal Family arrive at state banquets without evening gloves. While Queen Elizabeth would never have dreamed of not wearing a pair, both Queen Camilla and the Princess of Wales have forgone gloves for recent events, which probably spells the beginning of the end for the accessory. If gloves are worn, they are removed when eating and placed, folded, on the lap under the napkin.

The James Bond look: Black tie

This dress code, called 'black tie' or 'dinner jackets' on invitations, is the one most people will be familiar with in modern Britain – whether on red carpets, at cocktail parties, or even at some weddings (although one is at pains to flag that's an American import). It was deliberately created to be a less dressy form of white tie, although its origin is unclear. There is a lot of misinformation and conflicting stories. What we do know is that, in 1865, the Prince of Wales (Bertie) went to Henry Poole and Co. (a tailor that is still on Savile Row today) and ordered a 'celestial blue' silk dress jacket. This was a regular-length jacket that just covered the rump, with a relaxed fit and no horsehair inside. This new creation was ideal to wear when dining with family and close friends.

After this, it gets more complicated. Two Americans, James and Cora Brown-Potter, were invited by the Prince of Wales to Sandringham in 1886. It is said that James asked what he should wear and was sent by the Prince of Wales to Henry Poole, where a dinner jacket similar to the one made for Bertie was made for his dinner guest. The story then goes that after Sandringham, Brown-Potter wore his new dinner jacket back at his club in upstate New York, the Tuxedo Club, and the trend caught on and spread throughout New York City. A recent study, however, of the ledger of Henry Poole and Co. found there was no record of anything being made at all for a 'Brown-Potter'.

In another version of events, one told by our cousins across the ocean, it was at one of the Tuxedo Club's autumn balls that a number of the sons of members scandalised their parents by arriving wearing dress jackets without the tails. We know this bit to be true, as there is documented evidence that the more patrician members thought the fashion-forward younger generation looked 'like waiters'. One of the Dowager Countess of Grantham's most amusing scenes in *Downton Abbey* is when her son, Robert, arrives to dinner in black tie as his white tie has gone missing. She, too, believes he is a waiter. The members' club in upstate New York is why our friends in America call this dress code 'tuxedo'. But it is the next worst thing to being unpatriotic to use that term in Britain.

The male form of dress, like white tie, uses only two colours – black and white.* The key difference is that the dress shirt, while still white, has a turn-down collar. Today, winged collars are worn only for white tie. Button-down collars are totally wrong, however.

Many people get very animated over whether the marcella shirt should be fastened with visible dress studs, or whether a placket (a flap, basically) should conceal the shirt's fastenings. Trust the Brits to worry about this level of detail. You can do either, really, but a dress shirt with a placket is probably more correct by half an inch.

The bow tie should be black, hence the name. The bow tie hanging round the neck at the end of the evening is not as sophisticated as some people think. It's even less sophisticated when a fake one has been swapped out for a real one just to achieve that result. I shall pass on one of the best pieces of advice I have ever been given: get an outfitter to tie a proper bow tie around your neck, exactly measured to fit you. They can then unhook it at the

---

* Midnight blue is actually acceptable as well, although not seen very much any more. Remember the first dinner jacket for the then Prince of Wales was a 'celestial blue'. To the naked eye, this colour looks black but the softer colour often complements those with fairer features.

back, and you take it home and lay it flat in the wardrobe, ready to go for your next event. No more faff and stress trying to tie it as your taxi's pulling up outside.

Dinner jackets can be single-breasted with a peaked or shawl silk lapel, or double-breasted with a peaked lapel to suit the wearer's style. Wear a notched-lapel dinner jacket and be prepared for some around you to be visibly sick. White dinner jackets (or cream, usually) are only permissible in very tropical climates, as the lighter colour is thought to help reflect the heat. Britain is not one of those climates, so do not wear one unless you want someone to think you're bar staff. Whatever colour or cut of jacket you wear, it is never removed during the event.

Another sign of the changing times is the distinct lack of younger members of the Royal Family wearing cummerbunds. Whisper it quietly, but even I have lost mine and am not kept awake at night knowing I shall probably never wear it again. These pleated silk sashes are worn around the waist, pleats up, and are there to soften the break between the shirt and the trousers. If you are going without a cummerbund, fasten the jacket when standing.

Trousers for this evening look should only have one piece of braid down the outside of each leg, with patent pumps, dress shoes or very shiny black Oxfords on the feet.

The female form of black tie is harder, as so much depends on the type of event, time of year and personal preference. A good rule of thumb is that the more effort on the part of the host, the grander the dress. A simple cocktail party can mean a go-to LBD, but a gala birthday dinner with dancing will require something more lavish. If hosts have a preference on the length of dresses people wear, they should state it on the invitation or circulate it by word of mouth.

Unlike the male form, there is no need to wear black for the women. While it is perfectly acceptable to do so, dresses can be colourful or patterned. In fact, some say that the aim of those wearing just black and white is so those in dresses will stand out and look radiant.

Long hair can be worn 'down', or tied up if there will be dancing, as with white tie. Tiaras are not worn with black tie, however. Many wrongly think that a small evening bag with a thin strap will make them look like their mother or a maiden aunt, preferring a supposedly chicer clutch bag. These sorts are only making it diffi- cult when they are at drinks receptions, having to manhandle and balance a bag, glass of Champagne, a canapé, and also say hello to people.

Shoes, as for any form of formal evening dress, should ideally be closed-toe, but open-toed ones are becoming more acceptable for hotter weather and less formal events. But toenails need to be in immaculate condition and feet should be free of corns and bunions.

Ascot gavotte: Morning dress

This is the smartest daytime dress code, and due to the flurry of royal weddings, funerals and the Coronation, this flummery has recently been seen more frequently by the British public and the world than it usually would. Although other countries like Spain and the Netherlands still wear this on occasion, it dates back to our country and the short reign of Edward VIII, who introduced it as court attire, eschewing the older and more formal frock coat. It is also seen at Royal Ascot (though only for those in the Royal Enclos- ure), royal garden parties and more formal weddings. When Britain welcomes a visiting country for a state visit, we see our monarch and Royal Family in morning dress, which perhaps cements quite how British this dress code really is.

The cornerstone of the male form of the outfit is another tailcoat, but it is different from the one for white tie – a morning coat is single-breasted and curve-fronted, rather than cutaway at the waist. Most examples of this type of jacket are either black or charcoal grey, although dove grey is seen at Ladies' Day at Ascot,* and in 2022 dark navy was added – to some surprise – as an acceptable colour for Royal Ascot.

Felt or silk top hats may well be seen for this dress code, although usually only for outdoor events (they are compulsory for the Royal Enclosure). As 'men don't wear hats indoors', many choose not to wear one at all, as finding a place to store it can be a faff if there is no cloakroom.

The shirt is a regular shirt, often white, pale blue or pale pink, with a silk necktie of the wearer's choice. A foulard or cravat is not correct unless you want to look like you've ramraided Moss Bros.

Waistcoats are also worn, often low-cut and double-breasted, but single-breasted ones are fine. As with ties, they can be any colour to suit the personality of the wearer, but white, grey, buff or camel are the most popular choices. Novelty waistcoats with horses, dogs, flags or motorcars should be avoided. If the waistcoat is

---

* Sometime in the 1920s, Edward VIII, then the Prince of Wales, broke with tradition and wore a dove-grey coat made by his tailor, Frederick Scholte. George V was furious, as the court was in mourning for a distant relative. The lighter colour trend then took over and was reinforced by Cecil Beaton, who designed the costumes for *My Fair Lady*, and dressed the men in the Ascot scene all in dove grey.

single-breasted, it is still correct to leave the bottom button unfastened. Fastening it makes you look like an amateur. It is a courtesy that dates back to Edward VII, who was so corpulent he supposedly could not fasten the bottom button of his own waistcoat. His obsequious courtiers decided to follow suit so as not to fat-shame him, as it would now be termed. For double-breasted waistcoats, however, all buttons are fastened.

Breaking from a rule of all other types of formal dress, the trousers should not match the material of the coat. This is why we call this 'morning dress' and not 'morning suit', as nothing matches. Held up by braces and with a higher waist than more casual trousers, they are usually dark grey with a faint pinstripe, but they can also be checked or plain.

The shoes should be well-polished black Oxfords. Brogues or loafers just will not do.

The female form of morning dress has fewer codified rules, which – once again – makes it harder for those wearing it. But the context of the event matters here, too. The key is that, as noted, this is a daytime ensemble, so anything more suited to a corporate workplace or the evening (shiny materials, sparkling jewels) will look very out of place.

At the summit of the outfit is a hat. A proper hat always looks better, rather than a fascinator or an interesting hairpiece. Tongues wagged with outrage in 2011 when Samantha Cameron, wife of the then prime minister, dared arrive at the wedding of Prince William and Catherine Middleton with an emerald hairpiece rather than a hat. Many Brits felt that, while she looked great, as the wife of the head of government she should have followed convention and helped set the tone. If she were a regular guest, she may have got away with it.

That wedding was also the debut of two of the most bizarre pieces of millinery ever seen out of the context of a circus. The Princesses Beatrice and Eugenie each wore a Philip Treacy; one resembled an elaborate pretzel, and the other looked as if it had just about won a frenzied battle with a peacock. (It should be noted that the princesses were, latterly, excellent sports about it, and auctioned off the pretzel one for charity, raising a commendable £81,100.01.)

While ladies' hats are typically not worn after six o'clock in the evening, British weddings are somewhat of an exception. There, outfits are never changed unless there is a specific, lengthy break between the ceremony and the reception, and a separate dress code for the reception is specified, although that is now unusual outside of a royal context. Hats may be worn for the whole event (especially if prone to 'hat hair' after taking it off). This may mean that people wear their hats after six o'clock and when eating the wedding breakfast.

But hats for weddings should not be quite as voluminous as ones worn to fashion-forward events like Ascot. Presumably, as you will be sitting in pews or rows, the people behind you will curse you when your hat is so wide it obscures the action ahead. If a guest is ever in doubt as to whether to wear a hat, you can ask what the mothers of the couple getting married will be wearing for a steer, unless it is already specified on the invitation.

Dresses for morning dress can be colourful, and the material and length depend on the season and personal style. A tailored jacket worn over the top is correct for more formal events, and the hemline of the dress or skirt should not be above the knee. It is still not acceptable for anyone other than the bride to wear white to a wedding. Black should be avoided, too, unless you really hate the couple getting married and never wish to see them again.

Tights are correctly worn for formal dress in the UK, and shoes should again ideally be closed-toe and the heels not so high that the wearer gets a nosebleed.

Suit yourself: Lounge suits

While the rules of wearing these suits are more or less universal wherever you are in the world, we Brits have added our own layer of etiquette and some sartorial solecisms on top. This dress code, which can be worn at night or day, is most often now just called 'suits' or 'business dress' – but on invitations should be listed as 'lounge suits', as historically they would have been worn to lounge around in. Essentially the mid-nineteenth-century version of a tracksuit. (Heaven help the future of society if, in the year 2150, people are attending meetings in their Sweaty Betties.)

The style and panache of more recent British tailoring is largely thanks to George Bryan 'Beau' Brummell. He was, perhaps, the first 'influencer', as everything he wore seemed to suddenly become very fashionable. And his middle-class origins did not stop him from influencing what everyone from the Prince of Wales downwards would wear. Brummell introduced trousers (as opposed to knee breeches and stockings), along with darker and plain colours for suits. He also realised that it wasn't just women who wanted to look slender and elegant, and introduced the fitted look to jackets that we still wear today.

These darker colours are still correct. Sartorial snobs will recoil when someone wears a very light grey – or, worse, baby-blue – suit. Wear either with a pair of brown shoes and you should await deportation. For city wear, dark grey or dark navy are the two options available, although black suits are fine for funerals. Tweed and earthy-coloured suits are only for country pursuits.

The male form of the lounge suit involves a matching (material and colour) jacket and trousers, sometimes with a matching waist-coat, too, although unless exquisitely tailored, there is a danger you end up looking like a football manager. When standing, the jacket is fastened (top button only for two-button suits; middle for three-button) to give an automatically sleeker look. (It is only unfastened when seated, to put less strain on the poor button.) If only Boris Johnson and Donald Trump had remembered this more when they were in office. Although, granted, that was the least of their worries.

Students of the finer points of tailoring will know that British-style jackets have what are called 'double vents' on each side of the seat of the jacket, rather than a single vent in the middle, which is considered Italian style.

Shirts have turn-down collars but should not be button-down unless you are an American baby boomer. Around the neck is fastened a silk necktie, giving each wearer the chance to express their personality. Anything is possible, really, although Britain being Britain, there are rules on wearing certain patterns, as some denote a particular military regiment, members' club or school. Wearing such a tie design when you are in no way affili-ated to the organisation is likely to have you socially blackballed. If in doubt, avoid buying or wearing ties with diagonal stripes or crests. Whatever the design, the tie should stop where the trou-sers begin, which will vary depending on whether they are cut for braces (and sit a little higher) or for a belt (and sit on the waist).

For the female form for this dress code, again we are back to the mantra of 'context matters'. Generally, you want to strive to match the formality of the male form. This may mean choosing a smart dress, jumpsuit or skirt and blouse, or you may opt for trousers.

The key is the fabric choice and the style, matching it to the time of day and the occasion.

The length of skirt or dress depends on – you guessed it – the context, but generally something that stops just below the knee will be perfect. Jackets work well over dresses or blouses, especially in business settings to add a tailoring detail. A good-quality, fitted knitted cardigan is good, too, but may not be smart enough for all settings.

Higher heels are fine for most evening wear, but not for the office. Tights do not need to be worn if you don't want to, although they do add a touch of formality.

A sartorial contradiction: Smart casual

Brits are not known for dressing casually. Smart casual, itself an oxymoron, is about as successfully casual as many Brits can go. Once we get beyond this rung on the dress ladder, as a nation it collectively goes wrong.

You only have to walk down any street in any city or town in the hotter summer months to see what I mean. Perhaps there's too much flesh on display for the more prudish British disposition, or clothes that are a bit too tight and show our damp patches when the sun deigns to shine on us. Compare us to those who live in consistently warmer climes like Italy and Spain, and we are a shambles.

As you may have noticed, as each dress code gets less formal, there are fewer rules. Any coincidence then that the Brits struggle the less stringent the rules get and the more diffused the expectations? Some Brits even struggle to say this dress code's name, with people calling it 'smart caszh' to perhaps mask our awkwardness. In America, they have even renamed this 'business casual'.

So, if it is printed on an invitation, what does it mean? For both the male and female forms, the outfit is built around a jacket or some other type of tailoring. But not a suit jacket – a more relaxed jacket or blazer that is not part of a very executive matching set.

A smart pair of chinos, corduroys, moleskin trousers or even jeans is worn with the jacket – often, and most successfully, of a contrasting colour. While denim is very much at the more casual end of smart casual, a rip and tear-free pair should only be worn if you know the host won't mind you turning up to their bon vivant buffet with Michaelmas munchettes in a material that was first created for American farm workers.

The shirt is open-necked, but there should only ever be one button unfastened. Two buttons are acceptable if you are continental or on holiday outside of Britain, but three buttons and people will think you are a gigolo. Or Simon Cowell. (You can debate which is worse.)

Shoes can be brown, navy blue, or indeed any colour that suits so long as they are in good condition. Trainers are not appropriate.

The female form of smart casual again allows for more creativity, with a range of styles and fabrics available for the wearer to choose from. For more formal smart casual events, make sure there is a hint of tailoring to some element of the outfit, and that it all fits well. Great caution should be exercised that the outfit doesn't have too many 'soft lines' or fabrics that err too much towards lounge or athleisurewear.

You can wear trousers, but if not, hemlines of skirts and dresses should be on or below the knee. You can get away with wearing something that stops slightly above the knee if the context of the event allows and the rest of the outfit is on point.

Shoes are usually flat for this more relaxed dress code, or perhaps with a very low or wedge heel. Sandals are for beaches and hot climates, not for smart casual in Britain.

Dress codes and class

Whatever the dress code and outfit worn, to perhaps distinguish ourselves from other nations who may be wearing similar clothes, Britain has its own layer of indicators of social class when it comes to a person's wardrobe and accessories. To the relief of those who wear female forms of dress, most of these apply to male dress.

The old rule was 'men don't wear hats indoors', one of the tell-tale signs of a gentleman of 'good breeding'. With different attitudes to gender, this rule can perhaps be tweaked to 'certain types of hats shouldn't be worn indoors by anyone'. Baseball caps, beanies, fedoras, homburgs, top hats, bowlers, flat caps and Panama hats, for example, should be removed when a person transitions from outdoors to indoors. (The exception being department stores, air-port terminals and railway stations – as you are passing through those places, and not stopping.) But more structured, grander hats like the ones we see at weddings, Ascot and the like may be kept on the head – as they are part of the whole outfit (and perhaps held in place with hat pins) rather than an accessory.

Whatever the type of hat, know that in Britain, all hats must be removed by six o'clock. As the purpose of a hat is to protect the face from the sun, you can see why it would be looked at as laughable to see someone in a floppy beach hat at nine o'clock at night. Tongues will wag.

In the last ten years there has been a baffling resurgence in the popularity of tie clips (strips of metal to keep the tie attached to the shirt to stop it flapping). These have not only risen in popularity but have risen up the tie. Correctly, a tie clip should not be seen and should definitely not be visible when the jacket is fastened. The very practical and unshowy Philip, Duke of Edinburgh, used to use a nappy pin (hopefully one not previously used for actual nappies). His eldest son, Charles, often uses one too – but, like his father, has it towards the bottom of the tie.

Philip did, however, break one of the British class rules, when it came to his choice for the fold in the handkerchief in his jacket breast pocket. Folding the silk hanky into anything other than a plume is considered very gauche. (Look at photos of the King to see exactly how to do it.) While the straight-edge fold Philip did was probably more a reflection of his military proclivities, it was at least not as much of a solecism as having the corners of the hanky sticking out and visible. It's doubly bad if the design of the handkerchief and tie match.

Former prime minister David Cameron caused a twenty-four-carat hoo-hah when he once proclaimed that he didn't wear either a wedding band or a watch as 'gentlemen don't wear jewellery'. The idea amongst some upper-class people being that the less 'bling' a man wears, the more sophisticated. While that rule may have cut the mustard in the 1800s and 1900s, it's frankly chronologically careless not to wear a watch today, and the wedding band issue remains personal preference – for anyone. Historically, men started to wear wedding bands during the Second World War to remind them of home, whereas previously it was only women who wore wedding rings. Life is different now, and some people do, others don't. The Prince of Wales chose not to wear a wedding band when he married in 2011. His brother, the Duke of Sussex, chose the opposite.

The King wears a signet ring, however, on the little finger on the left hand. Signet rings are considered very smart, but there is a little-known code that in order for the wearer's ring not to be mocked, it must have the family crest on rather than initials. The King's has the Prince of Wales feathers – terribly chic!

The next rule gives us title of this chapter, and it's one I learned the hard way while on assignment in Barcelona in 2011. My colleagues Alexandra, Barbara and I had just finished the day's training to staff on a yacht and were disembarking to go and enjoy dinner in the city. I emerged wearing a pair of brown Oxford shoes, and Alexandra was so shocked at my choice of footwear that Barbara had to catch her from falling backwards into the marina. One really is not meant to wear one's browns in towns; they are solely for country wear. A black loafer would probably have gone better with my jeans and open-necked shirt that evening. (After that, I then decided to buy shoes in olive, powder-blue suede and purple, just to tease Alexandra – who, despite slagging off my shoes, remains a valued friend, colleague and mentor to this day.)

Brits with bags are less fussy than some of their bag-carrying counterparts from other shores. In the Middle and Far East, they often worry about placing their costly, designer bag directly on the floor, worrying that it will get scuffed. But in Britain, many just plonk their day bags on the floor, under the chair or beside them, with no worry. (The idea amongst the aristocracy is that worrying too much about a possession is vulgar and indirectly shows you don't have as much money as you think your bag of choice says you do.)

When viewed with a more compassionate modern lens, all of these shibboleths are faintly ridiculous. (Other ones to keep an eye out for are very light-coloured suits, wearing visible brands and brightly coloured nails.) A person's character, gentleness and generosity of spirit are much more valuable than how they've folded their pocket square. But they are fun to know and Britain just wouldn't be Britain without such indicators.

Town versus country

Styles and ways of dressing will vary greatly when it comes to dressing *au soir* for town and country. As is hopefully already obvious from this book, the Brits are always looking at ways to flabbergast foreigners with perverse rules, and one of these is that rustic, if not frumpy, country clothes will always be considered a surreptitious signal of being more 'U' than the finest threads from the city. Even now, at fashionable London parties and galas, dowdy dowagers from the sticks, dressed from head to toe in taffeta, still have the social edge over couture-clad WAGs of plutocrats and celebrities. And as ever with etiquette and manners, context matters. The skimpy little number from Browns that may very well be *sans pareil* in Mayfair will be dismissed as merely common in the Cotswolds.

In Britain, it was once a major transgression of taste for women to be seen in trousers after six o'clock in the evening. Until recently there was even a government-backed enforcement agency called OfCulottes who would police this very serious sartorial crime. Today, with most women having set aside their needlepoint and now in gainful employment, this rule is more or less obsolete and forgotten. There are, however, some older generations who still think trousers for ladies are only acceptable when walking dogs, sailing or gardening.

Once again we cite our favourite C-word: 'context'. Should you be invited to a ploughman's soiree in the country, then it may be best to opt for a skirt. Something heavily pleated in a mid-grey or an earthy colour should do the trick. You'll blend in nicely.

Black clothes, black comedy: Dress for mourning

When attending most funerals or memorial services in Britain, the expected dress is black.

If wearing lounge suits, the necktie should be black; the actual suit can be dark grey or dark navy, but can also be black, if you have one. Those wearing dresses should opt for something black, too, although avoid anything that looks too much like you are going to a cocktail party. While a staple of many people's wardrobe, the Little Black Dress is not as versatile when worn for mourning, unless demure and paired with a jacket and dark tights.

It is not just the clothes that switch to black when attending a funeral. Many Brits' humour becomes black, too. Those new to traditional British funerals should not be too alarmed if someone makes a faintly inappropriate joke, or finds a part of the sombre ceremony more amusing than it actually is. It is a British coping mechanism and part of our grieving process.

There has been a rise in funerals where the deceased has let it be known (before death) that they wish for mourners to wear bright colours in order to celebrate their life and be happy it happened, not sad that it is over. If that was their wish, it is good manners to go along with it, although purple is a good compromise colour if you find wearing anything but black a bit strange. Even a colourful silk handkerchief in the jacket pocket or another technicolour accessory would be better than refusing outright.

Highland dress

This alternative to formal British dress can be worn in Scotland as well as south of the border for certain appropriate occasions.

A Scot may wear a kilt at their wedding, even if it is not held in Scotland. But as a general rule of thumb, the kilt is not worn outside of Scotland unless the event is, by its very nature, Scottish – for example, the Royal Caledonian Ball held in London each spring. It may also be worn when 'national dress' is stipulated on the invitation.

The main piece for the male form of Highland dress is the kilt, which is worn higher than most trousers and should stop in the middle of your knee. It is fastened with a pin with a dress sporran, which can be real or fake fur. Real fur ones are considered acceptable if inherited or second-hand. Sporrans serve two purposes: as a handy purse, but also to preserve dignity by weighing the front of the kilt down. What to wear under the kilt is personal choice. Some will wear something, some will not. Hopefully the sporran is suitably stuffed to stop anyone finding out whether the wearer is with or without pants.

The shirt should be plain white, with either a black bow tie or a lace jabot (that's the correct term for 'like the frilly thing Mrs Slocombe used to wear in *Are You Being Served?*'). On top of the shirt is a Highland jacket (often called a doublet) with silver buttons. There are several styles (and if you are renting the outfit, knowing which style you want in advance is helpful), but they are normally made from a black or dark-coloured barathea, broadcloth or velvet. A waistcoat is not needed but is often worn.

Turning our attention now to below the sporran, the legs are clad in knee-length, green, red or patterned long socks. Cream hose is not ideal and a bit of a giveaway you've hired it. A *sgian dubh* (a small knife, pronounced 'ski-an doo') may be placed on the right-hand side – although, for any events where there is security due to higher-profile guests, it is best to leave it at home for want of an easy night. The shoes are black patent leather dancing pumps or any other form of black evening shoe, although they often have firmer soles to help with vigorous reeling.

A word of caution to those not from Scotland when shopping for your Scottish get-up. Several American jocks once went into an outfitter in Edinburgh to get their ensemble for their friend's Highland wedding. While they waited for the assistant to finish with the previous customer, they browsed the kilts, making stupid jokes about men in skirts and other pejorative comments.

The assistant noted this and, when it was their turn to be served, asked whether the American men needed regular kilts or the longer 'warrior kilts' for this wedding. Seizing on the opportunity to reinforce their clearly fragile masculinity, they asked for the warrior kilts. When they arrived at the wedding, they were perplexed to find all the other guests laughing at them. The sales assistant in Edinburgh had, knowingly, sold them midi-length lasses' kilts and had the last laugh.

Men who, for reasons of their supposed pride or modesty, do not want to wear a kilt, can wear tartan trousers called 'trews'. These are worn with a velvet smoking jacket and black bow tie and are always cut without a side seam.

For those dressing in the female form of Highland dress, especially when reeling is the order of the day, dresses are long, with a full skirt. At formal balls, dresses are often worn with a sash (though making any Miss World comments is misplaced). The tartan sash is worn diagonally, but the direction depends on your status. Clanswomen wear it over the right shoulder and across the breast, secured by a pin or small brooch on the right shoulder. The wife of a clan chief, or the wife of a colonel of a Scottish regiment, would wear a slightly wider sash over the left shoulder, secured on the left with a brooch. Non-clanswomen attending balls do not wear sashes.

Shoes for dresses should suit the occasion and any intended rhythmic gyrations. If reeling is on the cards, stiletto heels are totally unsuitable, and you may end up in Dunfermline A&E quicker than you can say 'gie her a haggis'. Any shoe should be well strapped to the ankle or foot, too, or else you run the risk of one flying off and hitting someone right in the middle of the Cairngorms.

Finally, before we leave the Highlands, a word on tartans. It is best not to wear a specific tartan unless connected to a specific clan. Many Scottish clans have one or more tartans – typically a dress tartan and a hunting tartan – which may be worn by members of that clan and their wives. Daughters may continue to wear it after marriage. For Highland balls, men who are not entitled to wear the kilt may wear black tie or, occasionally, white tie. As ever, ask the host if unsure.

Bare necessities: Modest dress

Modest dress is not just reserved for Muslim countries. Many people choose to dress more conservatively in parts of Britain and other countries, regardless of their religious beliefs. For example, when visiting Roman Catholic places of worship, modest dress should be worn.

Aside from the religious and cultural considerations, many countries where modest dress is required are very warm for much of the year, so it is advisable from a comfort point of view to keep clothes loose and be well-covered, which will also provide protection from the sun.

When overseas, especially in the Middle East, it is important to remember that what may be accepted in our home country may not be in another. Some countries are more relaxed than others, so prior research is needed, but it is always best to play it safe (and even safer when travelling during Ramadan*). It will only gain someone more respect if deference is paid to the local customs. This applies not only to the clothes worn when working, but in any free time the person may have in that country.

Avoid exposed torsos and shoulders, bare arms or midriffs, dresses above the ankle, tight or fitted clothing, swimwear (away from pools and beaches), translucent clothing, and do not show any part of your undergarments.

Aside from the standard rules for the male form of lounge suits and smart casual, you can wear long-sleeved loose tops, palazzo pants, long shirts, tunics, kaftans, capri pants and harem trousers. For ease in most Muslim countries, visiting ladies can wear an abaya (the cloak that is worn over other clothing that goes to the feet, often with a headscarf). But it is not correct for visiting men to wear the white thobe / dishdasha and head covering that Middle Eastern men wear.

---

* The dates for Ramadan change each year, so do not be caught out thinking that as it was in March when you last visited, it'll be March again for this trip.

CHAPTER NINE

Royal Standards

It would be next to impossible to write a book on British manners without mentioning the Royal Family. So much of our behaviour as a nation has come from court life, directly or indirectly. Our ideal national characteristics of charm, restraint and poise are represented in the monarch and their family. Although many Brits may protest and say otherwise, the good ones give us (and our global neighbours) a standard to which to aspire – with some of us more successfully achieving that standard than others.

This has been especially true during politically turbulent times, not just in the United Kingdom but elsewhere. While politicians bicker, squabble and let the side down, the British monarchy rises above the now-familiar ugliness of politics and remains a constant source of stability and comparative unity.

It was widely noted on social media at the time, but in the space of less than a week in September 2022, Britain changed both its head of state and head of government without much fuss, outrage or insurrection. Aside from being mannerly role models, the current system of constitutional monarchy allows for royalty to be a vehicle for current social concerns, to highlight causes and to champion the people in a non-political, non-partisan way. The monarchy takes up the slack and allows the three arms of the British government to function in a far healthier way.

If we were creating a country from scratch today, would we choose to install a monarchy? Probably not. But Britain is not a country that began the day before yesterday. We have one of the richest histories in the world, and our Royal Family goes back nearly as far as the nation.

During March 2024, social media and royal watchers reached a breathless fever-pitch obsessing over the whereabouts of Catherine, the Princess of Wales, who had taken a few months off after an operation. To me, this lunatic speculation and thirst to see one of the Royal Family's biggest assets showed just how much we as a nation want and need the royals to feel normal and like we, as a country, have everything together. How dare she take a break from the national stage for a valid medical reason? Perhaps if the world of politics were more stable, we might be less worried about the Royal Family's whereabouts and visibility.

And when our royalty is present, we as a nation can get very animated over their actions, prompting reams of column inches and fervent debate. I've never been busier than when Meghan, the Duchess of Sussex, dared to close her own car door when visiting the Royal Academy in 2018. I tell a lie – it was pretty full on in 2016 when the then Duchess of Cambridge dropped a water bottle and managed to pick it up all by herself.

How we interact with our head of state and their family has changed. Britain is no longer anywhere near as deferential as it was when Charles III's mother came to the throne in 1952. While we may be less impressed by the pomp and ceremony than we used to be, as documented by car doors, water bottles and less important moments like jubilees and the Coronation, Brits hold a very special place in our hearts for the Royal Family (even if many don't like to admit it). Probably because the alternative could be so much worse.

Bowing and scraping: Meeting royalty

Gone are the days when it was de rigueur to bow and scrape. Alas. I miss those days, as it was so elegant when done correctly. I am slightly biased as I hold a Guinness World Record for curtsying. Set in 2012, I was flown to New York City to teach a room full of businesspeople how to do the perfect royal curtsy to set the record for 'longest curtsy relay'. My parents are so proud.

Even the Royal Family's website remains very wishy-washy on the subject, offering the advice that 'there are no obligatory codes of behaviour – just courtesy', but then immediately below outlining how to bow and curtsy. As they say, many people do feel like they want to do something. It is important to remember that you are really genuflecting to the institution and not to the specific person.

Traditionally, men bow and women curtsy. But in more progressive days and with different attitudes to gender, anyone of any gender can do either option. Diana, Princess of Wales, always used to giggle when a nervous provincial mayor would drop into a low curtsy rather than a bow. If she were with us today, I doubt she'd find it that funny any longer and would rather champion it all. Whichever option you choose, try to make it look as natural as possible and not painfully forced or anxious.

Royal bows are not great big theatrical bows, with one hand sweeping across the body and the other out and back to the side. Nor are they regimented Japanese-style bows. British royal bows are much easier than that, with just a brief nod of the head from the neck. Similarly, curtsies are not the sweeping movements you may have seen in period dramas (as if you go down too low, you may never rise again); nor are they like little girls at ballet pulling out the edges of their dress. A perfect curtsy is a brief bob, one foot behind the other, with the weight on the front foot, bending the knees and nodding the head at the same time. Easy. For either movement, do not extend your hand to shake unless the member of the Royal Family extends theirs first. If you do shake hands, a standard British handshake of one or two pumps is fine. You don't over-pump queens.

If you happen to be a citizen of a country where the British Royal Family do not form your monarchy, then firstly, I am sorry. Secondly, be aware that although you do not have to bow or curtsy, many people still like to, especially when meeting the starrier members of the Royal Family. The former Australian prime minister Julia Gillard failed to do anything when meeting Her Majesty Queen Elizabeth on the latter's state visit in November 2011, and the former British prime minister's wife Cherie Blair was infamous for her lack of curtsying. Neither of these transgressions by two of her subjects noticeably fazed the late Queen, and neither should you be bothered if you notice anyone else petulantly refusing when they really ought to.

How to address the Royal Family

Starting at the top, we have Charles III and Camilla, the King and Queen. They are addressed first as 'Your Majesty' and then, after that, 'Sir' and 'Ma'am'. And yes, 'Ma'am' still rhymes with 'jam', as it is short for 'Madam'.* 'Madame' is very French and not heard in Britain, unless, perhaps, when shopping in a Chanel boutique.

The Prince and Princess of Wales are referred to as 'Your Royal Highness', again followed by 'Sir' or 'Ma'am'. The same form applies to the Duke and Duchess of Edinburgh, the Princess Royal, the Duke and Duchess of Gloucester, Princesses Alexandra, Beatrice and Eugenie, and the Duke and Duchess of Kent, Prince and Princess Michael of Kent.

How royal spouses are addressed varies depending on sex. Wives of male royal blood automatically assume their husband's title. For example, Sophie, the Duchess of Edinburgh (married to Edward, the Duke of Edinburgh). Upon marriage, she was granted Royal Highness status through her husband.

Husbands of women of royal blood are, alas, not given any elevated title, and so nothing changes in how we address them. Both Edoardo Mapelli Mozzi and Jack Brooksbank, respective husbands to Princesses Beatrice and Eugenie, remain styled as any other male in the UK with no professional or significant title. They can, however, be addressed as 'Sir', if you want.

Referring to the Royal Family

Our monarch is referred to as 'His Majesty' and/or 'the King' – or, perhaps only in writing, 'Charles III'. 'King Charles' is a bit tabloid and best avoided. His wife is referred to as 'Her Majesty' and/or 'The Queen' or 'Queen Camilla'. Those who bang on about how

---

* Only in the British police force do they pronounce 'Ma'am' to rhyme with 'farm'.

she won't ever be Queen in their eyes are best excluded from intelligent conversation as they have clearly created their own fantasy land in the echoey chamber inside their head.

Most other members of the working Royal Family are a Royal Highness and so styled as 'His/Her Royal Highness' when referring to them and then 'Your Royal Highness' in direct speech, followed by 'Sir' or 'Ma'am' according to sex. It is totally wrong to say 'Princess Anne' unless you have been transported back to 1987 or earlier. Similarly, 'Princess Kate' is not a thing and never will be, and saying 'Prince William' is again tabloid and inaccurate; they are referred to as 'the Prince and Princess of Wales'. Avoid referring to the Royal Family as 'the Royals' as – not to labour the point – it's just a bit common.

Conversation with the Royal Family

Dialogue with royalty suggests that you gracefully allow them to steer the topics and direction of the conversation. Asking direct questions used to be frowned upon, but today the rules are slightly more relaxed. During the reign of Elizabeth II, it was really bad form, but with a (slightly) more contemporary style of monarchy now emerging, this rule can be adjusted.

It is, however, still not good to ask anything that would require the member of the Royal Family to give a divisive opinion or offend anyone. For example, do not ask anything about other members of the family – persona grata or otherwise – or whether they enjoyed a particular part of a service.

Know your queens

During the reign of Elizabeth II (1952–2022), we addressed Her Majesty as any queen regnant would be addressed: 'The Queen'. But since her death on 8 September 2022, many people do not know what to call Britain's longest-reigning monarch.

Strap yourselves in, as this majestic explanation can get confusing.

After Elizabeth II died, Buckingham Palace decided to style Camilla, wife of King Charles III, as 'the Queen Consort' until the Coronation on 6 May 2023, to avoid confusion between the late Queen and the new Queen.

Before we go any further, however, let's clear up the differences between types of queens, as there are several, and I can feel the Diana fans starting to get riled up. We have regnant, consort and dowager queens. (There is also a queen regent, where a queen reigns in place of their underage child or absent husband, but we haven't had one of those since the reign of Henry VIII; and, thanks to the introduction of Counsellors of State in 1911, we are very unlikely to ever have one again.)

Queens regnant are female monarchs who reign over a realm in their own right. Elizabeth Alexandra Mary (1926–2022) was a queen regnant, and the second-longest reigning monarch in the world after Louis XIV. Other notable examples are Elizabeth I and Victoria. During their reign, queens regnant are called 'the Queen' (note no use of their first name).

A queen consort (today, this is Camilla) is married to a reigning king but does not share their husband's political or military power.

Other examples are Edward VII's wife, Alexandra, between 1901 and 1910, and George V's wife, Mary, between 1910 and 1936. During the reign of their husbands, queens consort are known as 'the Queen' or 'Queen FirstName'.

A queen dowager is a widowed queen consort, such as Queen Alexandra and Queen Mary, respectively, after Edward VII and George V died. Once widowed, queen dowagers are referred to as 'Queen FirstName' but not 'the Queen'.

All types of queens listed above get the 'Her / Your Majesty' styling for life.

Elizabeth II may now be called Queen Elizabeth or Elizabeth II. Informally, you can use 'the late Queen', which sounds warmer but will pass with time. But by switching to styling Britain's longest reigning monarch as 'Queen Elizabeth', we now encounter a problem.

After 1952, the late Queen's mother, who was born Elizabeth Bowes-Lyon, was referred to as 'Queen Elizabeth'. During both their lifetimes, to avoid confusing her with her daughter – who, after she acceded to the throne as queen regnant, was 'the Queen' – the Royal Household also attached 'Queen Mother' to the title (although this was reportedly never used in front of the Queen Mother). Thus, her title was 'Queen Elizabeth, the Queen Mother'. (Incidentally, if you are still with me, a queen mother is a type of queen dowager, where the person in question is the mother of a reigning monarch.)

Thus, how do we now distinguish between the two Queens Elizabeth? Elizabeth II is now referred to as such or 'Queen Elizabeth', and her mother should be 'Queen Elizabeth, the Queen Mother'. Wordy but correct.

Why is Camilla a queen, but Philip was never a king?

In essence, the answer is sexism. But that is when viewing the issue through a contemporary lens. To be a king, you have to inherit the title, and not be appointed one, and under Common Law, a king outranks a queen of any kind (regnant, consort or dowager). If Prince Philip had been made a king, he would have sat higher than his wife, then queen regnant, even if he was styled 'King Philip' and not 'the King'.

Camilla was crowned during the May 2023 Coronation service in a similar but simpler crowning to the King. Philip was never crowned or anointed during the 1953 service or else he would have outranked the monarch.

Harry, Meghan and Andrew

It speaks volumes about the British character that after Harry, Meghan and Andrew all stepped down from being working members of the Royal Family, for very different reasons, one of the key questions the British press and public had was 'But how do we address them?' There was a burning, impassioned concern for what happened to their titles.

Currently, the Duke and Duchess of Sussex are still, technically, Royal Highnesses but, following their stepping back from royal duties, their titles are not used unless in a legal setting. For Prince Andrew, the second son of Queen Elizabeth, who stepped back from his public role under a much darker and more serious cloud, his HRH status has been revoked for public use, although he reportedly still uses it in private, apparently with his late mother's blessing.

So, how do we refer to and address these assorted members of the Royal Family's rogues' gallery? In essence, no one really knows, and there is not a definitive answer from either the Royal House-hold or the parties in question. Common sense must take hold.

The men in question would now be addressed as 'Sir' and referred to as 'the Duke of Sussex' or 'the Duke of York'. Meghan would be addressed in conversation as 'Ma'am' and referred to as 'the Duch-ess of Sussex'. In the instances of meeting the Californian exiles, you may even be invited to use their first names, in which case it is correct to do so.

As they are no longer officially styled Royal Highness, you do not need to bow or curtsy to any of them unless you feel the urge. For whatever reason.

Royal dining rules

Frankly, the mechanics of how you eat at Buckingham Palace or Windsor Castle should be exactly the same as how you eat in a high-street restaurant. The only thing that changes is, to use theat-rical terms, the cast, costume and set. The company you dine with may be more prominent, the cutlery and linens of finer quality, and the food much tastier, but other than that, the manners needed are more or less a copy-and-paste job.

The only necessary nuance is knowing that you do not eat before the King (or the most senior member of the Royal Family present), and that ideally, as soon as the King has finished eating, everyone else must follow suit. This is a rule that gets trotted out and quoted in the British and international press every time there is a royal occasion to get excited about. It's a fun fact, but is actually not limited to the British Royal Family. The protocol is the same wherever you are in the world if a head of state is present, whether it's a royal or political one. Whether each royal or official residence enforces this rule in practice is, of course, another matter.

Writing to royalty

The old rule was that unless you were a close personal friend of the member of the Royal Family to whom you were writing, all letters should be addressed to their respective private secretary. In practice, most letters now are addressed directly to members of the Royal Family.

In February 2024, when Buckingham Palace's social media released a video thanking well-wishers for their messages to the King following his cancer diagnosis, the envelopes featured were all addressed directly to His Majesty, subtly marking a shift in royal protocol.

If opting for a direct approach when writing to the King or Queen, which years ago may have had you excluded from royal circles quicker than you could say 'Paul Burrell', the letter should start 'Sir', 'Madam' or 'May it please Your Majesty'. The first line of the body of the letter should begin with 'With my humble duty'. There then follows the main thrust of the letter. When ready to sign your name, it should end 'I have the honour to remain, Sir/Madam, Your Majesty's most humble and obedient servant'. (Some consider this to be a touch obsequious but, frankly, if you are writing to royalty I'd get over yourself pretty quickly and pick your battles.) The envelope should be addressed to 'His Majesty The King' or 'Her Majesty The Queen'.

When writing to those with a Royal Highness designation, the letter opens in exactly the same way but ends with 'I have the honour to remain, Sir/Madam, Your Royal Highness's most humble and obedient servant'.

In a flap: Flags

Although it may seem insensitive to laugh, one cannot help but – with hindsight – smile at the public fuss that was kicked up in September 1997 when Buckingham Palace did not initially fly a flag at half mast after the death of Diana, Princess of Wales. The stringent logic of the courtiers at the time was that the only flag to ever fly above a royal building was the Royal Standard, and only when the monarch was in residence. As Queen Elizabeth was at Balmoral, the Buckingham Palace flagpole remained empty. You would never fly the Royal Standard at half-mast as, thanks to the hereditary core of the monarchy, the monarch never dies, hence the saying 'The King is dead, long live the King'.

Here, you had two conflicting traits of the modern British character. The rule-followers who knew that the lack of any flag at half mast had no bearing on any private or mixed feelings towards Diana (if anyone else royal or previously royal had died, no flag would have flown, either), and the more emotional, reactionary brigade who knew that while the rule-book might say one thing, surely something should be done. (Both groups united over their strong feelings towards the issue of the monarchy.)

The compromise, which seems so obviously simple to us now, was to fly the national flag, the Union Flag, above Buckingham Palace and other residences at half mast, while the Royal Standard flew at full mast above wherever the Queen was. Since this vexillological vexation, the Royal Household now flies the Union Flag at full mast above most royal properties, unless the Monarch is in, in which case it gets switched for the Royal Standard, as per the usual custom. Since the reign of Charles III, the Royal Standard gets flown above both Buckingham Palace and Clarence House when His Majesty is in either. Which, while a necessity due to the ongoing renovations of the Palace, makes slightly more sense from a modern security point of view. Only in Britain would we drop any concern for the safety of the monarch, waving a great big brightly coloured flag pinpointing their exact whereabouts, in order to follow royal protocol.

The royal wave

Contrary to what the media or Instagram reels may tell you, there is no such thing as the royal wave. Members of our Royal Family are not hauled into a classroom to have the Princess Royal stand at the front and get them all to copy what she's doing until it becomes muscle memory. Each member of royalty does it differently and in their own style.

The only consistent trait of such a gesture is, much like British manners in general, it is something that is not too bold, in your face or strenuous. The Royal Family often has to wave for very long periods of time – horse-drawn journeys down The Mall, through Horse Guards Parade and down Whitehall. Waving frantically for the duration would play havoc with their wrists and mean they'd need to wrap them in ice by the time they took their seats at the Abbey or Houses of Parliament.

When the Duke of Windsor was Prince of Wales, he shook so many hands and waved to the crowds so much during a royal tour he had to have his right arm in a sling for the duration of the overseas visit, greeting people with his left hand.

It amused me greatly to see that en route from the Goring Hotel to Westminster Abbey on 29 April 2011, Catherine Middleton repeatedly waved to the thousands lining the streets in a manner that looked most tiring. Her hand swung all over the place, like an overenthusiastic child standing beside a railway line. It looked slightly undignified and distinctly un-royal. It was a miracle she didn't concuss her father beside her.

She emerged from the service, now styled Her Royal Highness the Duchess of Cambridge. During her return journey up The Mall, sitting alongside her husband in the state landau, the wave had become much more considered, restrained and fitting for the newest member of the Royal Family.

Conclusion

I suspect people will have had one of two reactions to this book.

If you are British by birth or have lived in the United Kingdom for long enough, you will not be surprised at much of what is contained in these pages. You may not have realised the origin of certain customs or have known all the rules, but – in broad red, white and royal blue strokes – you probably understood that Britons have a certain way of doing things that many other countries do not.

If you have not spent much time in Britain, you might find the manners we have baffling, complex or even faintly ridiculous. Some Brits don't do a good job of explaining to newcomers that there is a way of doing things; some don't listen.

Take the fuss that was created in the British press (who echoed the public) around the Duchess of Sussex announcing to guests at the wedding of Princess Eugenie and Jack Brooksbank that she was pregnant. There are hardly any etiquette books that state 'do not upstage the couple getting married with your own attention-grabbing news', so you could be generous and say Meghan was not to know and seized a convenient opportunity to tell her new family all at once while they were gathered under one roof. What's wrong with efficiency? Well, to the British, this was very poor timing and a lapse in common sense. We would usually prioritise process and form over anything else, especially self-interest.

During the writing of this book, I was asked to appear on the American podcast *Were You Raised by Wolves?* and I asked hosts Nick Leighton and Leah Bonnema what they thought the difference between British manners and those in other countries was. 'At their core, they are very similar,' Nick responded, 'but in Britain, there's definitely a more proper way to do things, and there are narrower parameters of what's considered "proper". In the US, there is a wider range: something can be considered formal and fancy and that can mean a lot of different things. Whereas in the UK, those parameters are a little narrower, which, on some level, makes it easier.'

Let's face it, most of us – wherever we are from – enjoy knowing what is expected of us at any given moment. Children thrive when faced with rules and structure, and their elders do, too. I would posit that the United Kingdom's manners may well be a form of protection: a polite way to defend and distinguish ourselves from outsiders as an island nation. They serve as both a protective barrier and a unifying force, subtly distinguishing the British identity from others. This safeguard of social codes helps us maintain a sense of decorum and distance in interactions, which can sometimes shield us from the unpredictability of unfamiliar customs and the anxiety they can induce.

Manners ensure a predictable, respectful exchange, minimising misunderstandings and potential conflicts. Our insistence on saying sorry for almost everything, even when it is not our fault, is a key example. We try to avoid a fuss and, in doing so, pepper our interactions with that appeasing five-letter word to diffuse any nastiness and tension. Perhaps, as we are such a small country, we have had to get along with those around us, as there aren't any nearby canyons, mountain ranges or plains in which to run and hide and start another community. Maybe our comparatively placid weather and the absence of having to panic about hurricanes, tornadoes, droughts and tsunamis means that we have become obsessed with the minutiae of manners as something to pass the time.

The King summarised these British traits in a speech at the Mansion House in 2023 as our 'deep well of civility and tolerance, on which our political life and wider national conversation depend, suffused with our sense of fairness'. Eloquently put, even if a number of world leaders and those in public life do need a return to the etiquette classroom.

At their core, manners are about treating others with respect and good grace. The novelist Dame Barbara Cartland called them 'invisible and indefinable', which I rather like. Thanks to the internet, smartphones and accessible international travel, we now have many more opportunities to interact with people from a wider variety of backgrounds.

In a firmer tone than when we began this exploration of modern manners, I would like to silence those who think we no longer need etiquette. Off with their heads, frankly. Standards of courtesy, tolerance and respect could and should be improved across society. British etiquette is still the finest in the world, and when you boil it down, it's just good manners.

Thank You

Firstly, to you, dear reader, for buying this book. Well, I hope you bought it, at least, as stealing is very bad manners indeed. Hopefully, you finish my offering a little bit politer than you were before. Not that you weren't polite to begin with. Perhaps I should have said 'even more polite than you were before'. Let's move on.

Since our first meeting in 2023, Harriet Poland at CAA Publishing has been ever-patient and understanding with my flapping, panic and angst. Thank you so much for being a brilliant and inspiring literary agent. Touring bookshops critiquing the covers and packaging of other books will forever be a highlight. I learned so much in one afternoon. Her colleagues Andrianna deLone, Alexandra Machinist, Erika Price and Agnès Rigou all get a big gold star, too.

Having not become totally bored by me while writing the *Help I Sexted My Boss* book, I must thank Zennor Compton for believing in me again and allowing me to write this, which has been a dream. This is the book I always wanted to write, and she and her colleagues at Century – Jessica Fletcher, Rachel Kennedy, Isabella Levin, Alice Gomer and Rose Waddilove – have made me so very happy and my publishing-to-date life dreamy.

Glenn Miller, Bilge Morden, Dan Rais, Camilla Dietrich, Barnaby Franklin and Georgia McHugh, from the other luxury divisions of CAA, have also supported me throughout the writing of this book.

Next, to Mikey Worrall, my husband, for putting up with my semi-detachment from social engagements and our own time together for the months it took me to write this. I owe him a trip to Miami, where I do not bring my laptop and let various etiquette books take up valuable case space in place of outfits he wants to wear. My parents, family and friends, too, have been nothing but understanding while I deflect invitations with the feeble excuse of 'I'm so sorry, but not until I've finished doing 300 words on stamps'.

Steven Moore has been, as ever, invaluable in assisting me with historical research in order to give this book some clout. He is so much more than the 'David Attenborough of teacups', and is – to many, and to me – a valued friend and colleague.

Sincere gratitude to everyone at The English Manner and our partner companies, including Bengt-Arne Hulleman, Diana Mather, Viviane Martins, Myka Meier, Alexandra Messervy, John Robertson and Jean Paul Wijers, but a special thanks to Jo Bryant, Eileen Donaghey and Anna Kirkman for holding the fort while I disappeared to the very edges of the team's radar to write this. Jo has also helped me with an 'etiquette edit' on the book, gently and lovingly chastising me when she felt I was being too strong on my stance towards soup spoons.

My thanks too to Freddie Northcott for his assistance on my social media, getting word of the book out there and (in the words of my husband) 'being more William than William'. Alex Barnes and John-Paul Stuthridge were also key to launching this book.

My *Sexted* colleagues, Jordan North, Stuart Morgan and Ben Cartwright, must also get a special mention, as without them this book (probably) wouldn't have been commissioned by Century in the first place.

For the research for this book, I am grateful and lie prostrate with praise to Ruth Baxter at Smythson, Ashley Coates, Andrew

Farquharson, Matt Ives, Oscar Lee, Charles MacPherson, Ella Robertson McKay, Viviane Neri, Joe O'Brien, Tom Sander, Jonathan Vernon-Smith and Jo Walters. They have all been generous with their time, experience and knowledge to help perfect this book, which I sincerely hope you have enjoyed reading as much as I have writing it.

Bibliography

Barr, Luke, *Ritz and Escoffier: The Hotelier, The Chef and the Rise of the Leisure Class*, 2018

Bryant, Jo, et al., *Debrett's Handbook*, 2015

Cartland, Barbara, *Etiquette Handbook: A Guide to Good Behaviour from the Boudoir to the Boardroom*, 2008

Crisp, Quentin, *Manners from Heaven: A Divine Guide to Good Behaviour*, 1985

Fox, Kate, *Watching the English: The Hidden Rules of English Behaviour*, 2004

Healy, Alicia, *Wardrobe Wisdom: How to Dress and Take Care of Your Clothes*, 2018

Lady Troubridge, *The Book of Etiquette*, 1926

MacPherson, Charles, *The Butler Speaks: A Return to Proper Etiquette*, 2013

Mikes, George, *How to be a Brit*, 1986

Mitford, Nancy, *Noblesse Oblige*, 1956

Morgan, Joe, *Queuing for Beginners: The Story of Daily Life from Breakfast to Bedtime*, 2008

Morgan, John, *Debrett's New Guide to Etiquette and Modern Manners*, 1996

Meier, Myka, *Modern Etiquette Made Easy: A Five-Step Method to Mastering Etiquette*, 2019

Post, Emily, *Etiquette in Society, in Business, in Politics, and at Home*, 1922

Scott, Andy, *One Kiss or Two? In Search of the Perfect Greeting*, 2017

Index